"Just Give Him the Whale!"

"Just Give Him the Whale!"

20 Ways to Use Fascinations, Areas of Expertise, and Strengths to Support Students with Autism

by

Paula Kluth, Ph.D.

and

Patrick Schwarz, Ph.D.

·P·A·U·L·H·
BROOKES
PUBLISHING CO.®

Baltimore • London • Sydney

Paul H. Brookes Publishing Co.
Post Office Box 10624
Baltimore, Maryland 21285-0624
USA

www.brookespublishing.com

Manufactured in the United States of America by
Sheridan Books, Inc., Chelsea, Michigan.

Cover illustration by Justin Canha.

Library of Congress Cataloging-in-Publication Data

Kluth, Paula.
   Just give him the whale!: 20 ways to use fascinations, areas of expertise, and
strengths to support students with autism / Paula Kluth, Patrick Schwarz.
      p.   cm.
   Includes bibliographical references and index.
   ISBN-13: 978-1-55766-960-5 (pbk.)
   ISBN-10: 1-55766-960-0 (pbk.)
   1. Autistic children—Education—United States. 2. Autism—United States.
3. Curriculum planning—United States. I. Schwarz, Patrick. II. Title.

LC4718.K577 2008
371.94—dc22   2007031481

British Library Cataloguing in Publication data are available from the British Library.

2012   2011   2010   2009   2008

10   9   8   7   6   5   4   3   2   1

Contents

Fascinations, areas of expertise, and strengths can be used . . .

About the Authors

Paula Kluth, Ph.D., is a consultant, teacher, author, advocate, and independent scholar who works with teachers and families to provide inclusive opportunities for students with disabilities and to create more responsive and engaging schooling experiences for all learners. Her research and professional interests include differentiating instruction and supporting students with autism and significant disabilities in inclusive classrooms.

Paula is a former special educator who has served as a classroom teacher, consulting teacher, and inclusion facilitator. She works with teachers in K–12 schools, preschools, and early intervention programs. She also regularly works with family organizations and disability-rights and advocacy groups. She is the author of *"You're Going to Love This Kid!": Teaching Students with Autism in the Inclusive Classroom* (Paul H. Brookes Publishing Co., 2003); the lead editor of *Access to Academics for All Students: Critical Approaches to Inclusive Curriculum, Instruction, and Policy* (with Diana Straut and Douglas Biklen; Lawrence Erlbaum Associates, 2003); the coauthor of *Joyful Learning: Active and Collaborative Learning in Inclusive Classrooms* (with Alice Udvari-Solner; Corwin Press, in press); and the coauthor of *You're Welcome: 30 Innovative Ideas for the Inclusive Classroom* (with Patrick Schwarz; Heinemann, 2007). More information about Paula can be found on her personal web site: http://www.paulakluth.com.

Patrick Schwarz, Ph.D., is Professor of Special Education and Chair of Diversity in Learning and Development for National-Louis University, Chicago. Patrick is also part-time Human Services Director for UCP Infinitec of Greater Chicago, in addition to presenting and consulting worldwide through Creative Culture Consulting. His books *From Disability to Possibility: The Power of Inclusive Classrooms* (Heinemann, 2006) and *You're Welcome: 30 Innovative Ideas for the Inclusive Classroom* (Heinemann, 2007), both cowritten with Paula Kluth, have inspired teachers nationwide to reconceptualize inclusion in ways that help all children.

Patrick's professional focus is furthering education and services that promote the status of individuals with a range of support needs. He works to facilitate successful engagement in various environments, allowing people to make contributions and develop experiences that are meaningful to them.

About the Cover Artist

As a child, Justin Canha's verbal communication skills were compromised, and he would draw different scenarios to express what had happened to him. Soon, Justin's parents discovered that he had been blessed with an innate artistic talent. Since age 5, Justin has had a passion for drawing animals and cartoon characters. At age 9, Justin won Best in Show for Cartooning, competing with students from kindergarten through high school in Palm Beach County, Florida. In time, he expanded his repertoire to encompass still-lifes, landscapes, portraits, buildings, and florals in a variety of media, including watercolors, pastels, charcoal, and oils. Also, Justin taught himself how to create computer animations, some having up to 200 frames per cartoon.

In September 2002, Justin and his family moved to Montclair, New Jersey, where he has been fully included in school with the appropriate supports. Justin has excelled in this environment and enjoys interacting with others, especially through his artwork. He loves to talk about his art—and particularly his comics—with whoever is interested.

Justin first appeared on the New York art scene in the well-received Autism/Aspergers Art Exhibit in January of 2005. Since then, Justin's career has been steadily gaining momentum. He received an Honorable Mention at the Studio Montclair Taboo Exhibition, which was juried by Jerry Saltz of *The Village Voice,* and portions of his animations were recently incorporated into a hip-hop music video. Justin's work has also been shown at the Beacon Firehouse Gallery in Beacon, New York; Montclair State University; Montclair's Luna Stage Theatre; The Cooper Union in New York; and the Rhode Island Convention Center in Providence. In addition, Justin had solo exhibits at the Montclair Public Library, at Pace University, and most recently at the JCC in Manhattan. In January 2008 his work will be featured at the Ricco/Maresca booth at the Outsiders Fair in New York.

Justin's artwork has been featured in *Sidecars,* a short documentary by Ben Stamper, and in *Autism: Communicating in a Different Way,* a documentary by Gary Keys. It also was shown in the August 2006 issue of *O, The Oprah Magazine.*

For more information on Justin and to see more of his artwork and his animations, visit his web site: http://www.justinart.com.

A Note About Terminology

Throughout this book, we often use *autism* to represent all labels on the autism spectrum, including Asperger syndrome, pervasive developmental disorder (PDD), childhood disintegrative disorder, and Rett syndrome. In doing so, we acknowledge that people with these labels don't necessarily experience them identically and that labels themselves are not discrete or exact. In addition, we use the word *labels* instead of any other term because we want to emphasize that categories on the "autism spectrum" are subjective and socially constructed and, therefore, are "things" assigned to people, not realities. Thus, we feel it is up to people on the spectrum to choose a label for themselves and to decide if autism, for them, is a disability, an attribute, an ability, a gift, a challenge, all of these, or none of these.

Introduction

I believe Autism is a marvelous occurrence of nature, not a tragic example of the human mind gone wrong. In many cases, Autism can also be a kind of genius undiscovered.

—Jasmine Lee O'Neill (1999, p. 14)

Many individuals with autism and Asperger syndrome have deep interest in one or a variety of topics. Stephen Shore (2001), a man with Asperger syndrome, shares that at some point in his life, he has been fascinated by airplanes, medicine, electronics, psychology, geography, watches, astronomy, chemistry, computers, music, locks, shiatsu, bicycles, mechanics, hardware, rocks, cats, yoga, earthquakes, electricity, tools, geology, dinosaurs, and autism.

Some people on the autism spectrum appear to share certain fascinations (e.g., trains, machines, weather, computers). Other fascinations seem to be more rare and specific to individuals. For instance, Sean Barron, a man with Asperger syndrome, reported that he once had a deep interest in the number 24 and at another point in his life, he became fascinated by dead-end streets (Barron & Barron, 1992).

Often, a student's educational team will focus on curbing a student's involvement with these interests or fixations. Many a meeting has been planned and a behavior program written to squelch a student's "obsessions." In some of these instances, the student may not even be aware that the decision to limit or eliminate the fascination has been made. Therefore, he or she may be confused or distressed when a favorite object or topic is banned or significantly restricted.

Liane Holliday Willey (2001), author, parent of a daughter with Asperger syndrome, and an "Aspie" herself, cautions that it can be dangerous for people without autism to pass judgment about interests and obsessions. In fact, she shares that in many ways and in many circles, having intense interests is considered positive and even admirable:

> At the base, I have to wonder, are we so very different from marathon athletes, corporate presidents, bird watchers, or new parents counting every breath their newborn takes? It seems lots of people, NT [Neurotypical] or

otherwise, have an obsession of sorts. In my mind, that reality rests as a good one, for obsessions, in and out of themselves are not bad habits. There is much good about them. Obsessions take focus and tenacious study. They are the stuff greatness needs. I have to believe the best of the remarkable—the artists, musicians, philosophers, scientists, writers, researchers and athletes— had to obsess on their chosen fields or they would never had become great. (p. 122)

Similarly, Luke Jackson (2002), a young man with Asperger syndrome, criticized the idea that it is okay for people without disability labels to have deep interests but that this is not okay for people with labels:

I have a question for teenagers here.
Q: When is an obsession not an obsession?
A: When it is about football.
How unfair is that?! It seems that our society fully accepts the fact that a lot of men and boys 'eat, sleep and breathe' football and people seem to think that if someone doesn't, then they are not fully male. Stupid! (p. 47)

Jackson goes on to point out how rigid society is when it comes to issues of difference and normalcy:

I am sure if a parent went to a doctor and said that their teenage boy wouldn't shut up about football, they would laugh and tell them that it was perfectly normal. It seems as if we all have to be the same. Why can no one see that the world just isn't like that? I would like everyone to talk about computers all day actually, but I don't expect them to and people soon tell me to shut up. (pp. 47–48)

We agree with Willey and Jackson and feel strongly that if educators could reframe obsessions as fascinations, passions, interests, or enthusiasms (Park, 2002) and see them as potential tools, educators and their students may potentially be more satisfied, calm, and successful. In fact, it is our opinion that students' areas of interest can be of tremendous help to teachers, and that is our reason for writing an entire book on this topic.

It should be noted, however, that even though we have always felt it important to respectfully negotiate with students and honor their uniqueness in any way possible, the idea for writing this book came not from a conversation we had with one another but from a conversation we had with Ms. Gomez, a principal of a Chicago public school. This wonderful school leader attended a meeting on inclusive schooling that we (the authors) chaired together. A committed group of advocates, teachers, parents, and administrators had come together to create a plan for an inclusive school and at one point, we began discussing how schools need to be more sensitive to the needs of learners with autism. Ms. Gomez nodded vigorously in agreement. She then told this story:

> Pedro, a little boy with autism, was screaming in his kindergarten classroom on the first day of school. Ms. Gomez, the principal, heard the child's cries and walked into the room. She observed two colleagues discussing the appropriate way to deal with the situation. It appeared that Pedro had started crying because the kindergarten teacher had taken away his favorite whale toy. Believing that her new student would be more successful without the "distraction" of his favorite possession, she had decided to try and hide it from him. The teacher's co-teaching partner, a special education teacher, had a different perspective on the situation. "What do you want him to do?" she asked her colleague. "I want him to do his work. I want him to participate," answered the kindergarten teacher. The special education teacher thought for a minute and replied, "Then just give him the whale."

We loved this story, especially when Ms. Gomez told us that soon after the incident, the children in the kindergarten class began bringing Pedro photos of whales to cheer, support, and connect with him. The kindergarten teacher, for her part, began incorporating whales into her lessons, examples, and classroom environment (e.g., reading whale stories, using whale stickers on worksheets).

The just-give-him-the-whale story became a centerpiece of our discussions for the next few days. We thought it was such a great metaphor for an ideology that, if adopted in schools, could change the ways in which students are perceived, curriculum and instruction are developed, and supports are designed. This small and simple book was written in response to that story, in celebration of Ms. Gomez and others like her, and out of respect for our friends and colleagues with autism who have been trying to tell us and show us for so long that human diversity is good for the community and good for the classroom. Interests *can* sometimes be limiting, but they also can be freeing, calming, motivating, captivating, and inspiring. In these pages, we hope to communicate that the fascinations, interests, and areas of expertise that are so often important to students with autism (and other students as well) should be valued, honored, and respected and used as a tool to teach, support, and include students in the classroom.

Acknowledgments

We are grateful to the many people who supported us to complete this project. Above all, we are most indebted to the many students with *possibilities* who have challenged us, taught us, and, of course, welcomed us into their lives over the years. We have been educated by many wonderful young people including Paul, Jason, Franklin, Tim, Mark, Jamie, Libby, Susan, Joe, Adam, Matt, Aaron, Andrew, and Bob.

And we are overwhelmingly grateful to our loved ones for supporting us and for allowing us time and space to do the work we love. Thank you Todd, Erma, Willa, Mary, Peggy, Victoria, Vicky, Tim, Sarah, Bob, Katie, and Haley. You all get it! Our close friends and colleagues have also been witness to and supportive of our soapbox at any given time; therefore, we pay tribute to Alice, Sandy, Buck, Kassira, Raul, Tanita, Howard, Tracy, Aria, Eileen, and Kaitlynn.

We are also in debt to the many individuals with autism who have shared their stories via conference presentations, research, and autobiographies, including Jamie Burke, Tyler Fihe, Temple Grandin, Kenneth Hall, Stephen Hinkle, Luke Jackson, Wendy Lawson, Eugene Marcus, Barbara Moran, Tito Mukhopadhyay, Jerry Newport, Jasmine Lee O'Neill, Sue Rubin, Jenn Seybert, Stephen Shore, David Tammet, Liane Holliday Willey, and Donna Williams. Through their words and shared experiences, we have learned to see differently and celebrate the fascinations of our students.

Justin Canha, the incredible artist whose work graces this book's cover, also deserves a public thank you. We have been in awe of his body of work for years, and when we asked him to create a piece of art for this book, we couldn't believe our luck when this busy young man agreed. Thank you so much for this gift, Justin.

And almost last, but not least, we send a big "we could not have done it without you" to the Christopher L. and M. Susan Gust Foundation, the Audubon School (especially Susan, Sheila, and John), and Pedro's fantastic support team (especially "Ms. Gomez"). These folks are responsible for the energy behind "just-give-him-the-whale," and they live this way of thinking every day in Chicago Public Schools.

Finally, we send our gratitude to all at Paul H. Brookes Publishing Co., especially Rebecca Lazo, who thought a little book about Pedro's whale was worthy of publication.

*To Pedro,
the lessons you taught
will serve and inspire many*

To Develop a Relationship with the Student

One of the most common ways to get to know another person is to exchange information about interests. Whether you are a scuba diver or a cat lover, chances are you look for opportunities to tell others about your area of specialty. Some of us even go so far as to "advertise" our (sometimes very unique) interests via T shirts, bumper stickers, tote bags, and coffee cups (e.g., "Baseball Isn't Everything, It's the Only Thing"; "I Love Beagles"; "Quilting Queen"). We share this information perhaps because we hope to start conversations with others about our favorite topics. Or maybe we are seeking those with similar fascinations. Or we may simply be asserting "This is who I am—this is something special about me." Asking students about their favorites is a great getting-to-know-you strategy. Because many students with autism have fascinations that may be unusual and not shared by many other people—like our friend, Jack, who loves wrenches—they may be especially appreciative of those who will take some extra time to listen and learn.

A formal way to use student interests to develop a relationship is to interview a student (or his or her family, if the student does not have a reliable communication method) about his or her area of interest. For example, Kip, a student who loves tractors, was shocked when his teacher, Mr. Rye, invited him to lunch and proceeded to ask him all about John Deere, Case, and other companies that the student revered. This was a turning point in Kip's education, as no teacher had ever treated his love of farm equipment as anything more than a tolerable quirk. Although Kip was never punished for talking about tractors, he was discouraged from doing so. As a result, he felt frustrated at school and routinely begged his mother to let him stay home. After being interviewed by Mr. Rye, however, he became excited to go to school and his mother reported that he worked harder for Mr. Rye than he had for any other teacher. When Mr. Rye asked Kip to take risks or to challenge himself, the young man would take the charge seriously and work to impress his teacher. When asked the reason for his turnaround, Kip replied, "I work well with Mr. Rye. We both love tractors. We understand each other."

Additional Ideas for Developing a Relationship with the Student via Interests or Passions

★ Take a tip from Mr. Rye and invite a learner to lunch or to a quick before-school breakfast meeting. Allow the student to tell you about his or her area of interest and to bring related pictures or artifacts. Be ready to ask questions and prepare to learn something new!

★ Survey the students in your classroom to learn about their areas of skill, interest, prowess, and talent. Use this information to build connections with learners and to help them build connections with one another. Be sure to adapt the survey to meet the needs of the various learners in your classroom. Questions can be open ended (e.g., "What are some of your favorite things?"), or you can offer a list of written options that can be circled or underlined beneath a heading that asks, "Which activities do you enjoy?" Students who do not have reliable communication will need a tool they can complete with support. These learners might be take a survey by using an augmentative communication device or by using a low-tech option such as choosing photos that represent special interests, activities, or things. See the end of this chapter for sample surveys.

★ Bring your own interests into the classroom. Part of building a classroom community is sharing of oneself. What better way to model this behavior than to disclose your own penchant for making and collecting model airplanes, participating in extreme Frisbee tournaments, or baking pies? Some teachers simply share stories with their students. Others bring in photos or even videotapes of experiences related to their passions. One teacher we worked with kept a scrapbook in her classroom that detailed her travels to rainforests. Students were welcome to peruse the book at any time and leave comments in the "guest book" section.

Sample Student Survey

Early Elementary Students

ABOUT ME

Draw a picture of yourself doing something you love.

What do you do for fun?

__ Play with friends

__ Play with my pet(s)

__ Make art projects

__ Play sports

__ Play on the computer/play video games

__ Read books

__ Ride my bike/play outside

__ Other: _____

What is your favorite part of the school day?

__ Reading/language arts

__ Math

__ Social studies

__ Science

__ Physical education (PE)/gym

__ Art

__ Music

__ Recess

What are your talents? (Choose one or more.)

__ Drawing/art	__ Sharing	__ Building things
__ Playing sports	__ Taking care of animals	__ Singing/dancing
__ Telling stories	__ Collecting things	__ Playing music
__ Making friends	__ Helping others	__ Telling jokes
__ Cooking	__ Pretending	__ Doing magic tricks

__ Other: _____

Draw a picture of a fun day at school.

Sample Student Survey

Late Elementary and Secondary Students

ABOUT ME

What words describe you best?

What hobbies do you have?

What do you want to learn this year?

What is your favorite part of the school day?

What is your favorite thing to do at school?

What are your talents or areas of expertise (e.g., karate, babysitting, collecting bugs, drawing)?

What else do you want me to know about you?

To Expand
Social Opportunities

Some students who find conversation and common methods of social interaction a challenge are amazingly adept when the interaction occurs in relation to an activity or a favorite interest. For instance, Patrick, an eighth-grader, had few friendships and seldom spoke to his classmates until a new student came into his English classroom wearing a Star Wars T shirt. Patrick's face immediately lit up and he began bombarding the newcomer with questions and trivia about his favorite film. The new student, eager to make a friend, began bringing pieces of his science fiction memorabilia collection to class. Eventually, the two students struck up a friendship related to their common interest and even formed a lunch club where a handful of students gathered to play video and board games related to science fiction films.

Another powerful example of activity-inspired relationships is shared in *Smiling at Shadows* (Waites & Swinbourne, 2001), the warm and candid memoir of an Australian family. Junee Waites, the mother of a young man with autism, shares a story of how her son's love of cycling led to many valued social connections. Initially, cycling was simply a personal hobby for Dane. He rode with his family and in much of his free time. Soon, however, he joined a cycling club, began entering races, and found he was able to develop a durable network of friends through the sport and its related activities (Waites & Swinbourne, 2001). Because making friends had been a struggle in Dane's life, his family was understandably nervous as he started his foray into the world of bike clubs and competitions, but these feelings of anxiety were allayed during the first big event Dane entered. As Dane's mother recounted, the experience was one to remember for Rod, Dane's proud father:

 Anxiously [Rod] watched as Dane lined up on his mountain bike, took off at the sound of the starter's gun, and rode through the town and out of sight. Other competitors joined the race then, the professionals at the rear attracting the most attention.

Unpleasant scenes began to play on Rod's mind as he walked around [waiting for the race to end]. What if Dane had a fall? Would he become disoriented and lose his way?

The professional riders roared home first. After this burst of excitement Rod positioned himself to await the amateurs. As the loudspeaker announced their imminent arrival he scanned the horizon with mild interest, thinking he wouldn't be seeing Dane for some time. To his utter astonishment there was Dane pedaling furiously over the crest of the hill and down the road. (p. 187)

Rod remembers seeing only "this huge smile on a bicycle." Tears poured down his face as he watched his son's finish. As powerful, however, was the sight of the riders gathering afterward to relax with a cold drink. Without hesitation Dane joined them; they laughed, patted him on the back, and exclaimed, "We saw you out there on the highway! You were going for it, mate!" (p. 187). Not only, then, did the experience give Dane a boost in confidence but it also gave him a way to connect with others who had a passion for cycling.

Both of these examples are important because many students with autism are accused of being antisocial or disinterested in building relationships. Although some individuals undoubtedly seek time alone and do not find all social experiences satisfying, many people with autism labels do crave interaction and relationships but need accommodations in this area. Some may need changes in the environment to successfully socialize (e.g., less noise), others may prefer to interact in relation to an activity (instead of sitting down for a face-to-face conversation), and still others, like Patrick and Dane, may want to connect to others in relation to their interests. Jasmine Lee O' Neill (1999), a woman with autism, suggested that any fascination can be used as a catalyst for a relationship:

 Use things the autistic individual enjoys to spark her interest. If she likes music and hums to herself, use music as an introduction to relating to other people. It is a falsehood that autistics do not relate. Rather, they relate in their own ways. (p. 83)

The notion that people relate in their own ways reminds us of Glory, a woman we have known for years. Glory has autism and is largely nonverbal. When we met her, we were told that her only "hobby" was manhole covers and that she was not interested in people, only in objects. When Kathy, a caring neighbor, began working with her, however, that assumption was put to rest.

Glory's favorite pastime was taking manhole-cover-walks through her neighborhood. Kathy would follow Glory as she weaved her way through the city blocks, located covers, and strolled around them leisurely. After a few weeks of engaging in the walks,

Kathy not only found that she valued the quiet experience (as Glory tolerated no talking during this activity) but also began to see how social her new friend intended the experience to be. Glory always grinned widely when Kathy came over and scurried to put on her sandals. As the weeks went on, she began to walk closer and closer to Kathy and even began to point to interesting sights in the parks and throughout the neighborhood. Kathy found that Glory seemed to be using the walks to get not only much-desired peace and quiet in her life but also perhaps something even more valuable—the undivided attention of a friend.

Kathy's hypothesis is bolstered by the words and experiences of Dawn Prince-Hughes (2004), a woman with autism and author of the autobiography *Songs of the Gorilla Nation*. Prince-Hughes recalled that one of her most cherished memories of being with her mother was taking a walk with her in a Florida park. Although the family engaged in all of the typical Florida family vacation activities such as taking a ride through the Everglades and visiting the Kennedy Space Center, it is walking silently through trees with a loved one that stood out in her mind:

We explored a trail near our campsite and found an almost mystical glade; showers of sun rained through the green of a canopy far above our heads. The trail wound in no hurry among the feet of trees and humble, concentrating rocks. I don't remember talking. We took turns swinging on a vine that hung between two trees. We laughed.

The entire time we were there probably didn't exceed twenty minutes, but it stands out as one of my favorite memories of my mother. I think that being outside where I felt safe, the absence of dialogue, and being alone with her allowed the walls around me to disappear so that I really connected with her deeply. (p. 38)

Additional Ideas for Expanding Social Skills and Opportunities via Interests or Passions

✦ Conduct a survey of the extracurricular options in the student's school. Is a broad range of options available? Are choices offered for students with different needs, strengths, and interests, or are choices primarily for the athletic, outgoing, and academically talented? Might new options need to be created to meet the needs of a wider range of students? Ask students if they have ideas for new clubs or organizations.

✦ Determine whether the student's area of strength is something that he or she could teach to someone else. Could structured opportunities be engineered for the student to show others what he or she knows or even to tutor classmates in learning a new hobby or interest?

✦ Use the Internet to explore ideas for connecting the student with others who enjoy his or her passions. It may be hard to find a handful of students in your school who want to constantly discuss the Enola Gay, its crew, and its mission, but there are plenty of military men and women, history buffs, and airplane lovers who do just that in chat rooms and in electronic communities every day. Although teachers and families certainly need to take the usual safety precautions (and teach these precautions to the student) for using the web, the Internet can be a nice social supplement for those who enjoy ways of interacting that are a bit less direct and require few traditional social skills.

To Expand Communication Skills and Opportunities

$\mathcal{C}$ommunication goals are almost always a focus of the educational programs of students with autism and Asperger syndrome. Individuals may have problems in any number of areas, including pragmatics, semantics, and language processing. No matter what difficulties the learner is experiencing, however, favorites can often be used to support new skill acquisition and the development of new competencies.

For example, Devon, an eighth-grader who needed to practice using a communication device, struggled to do so when Ms. Rice, his speech therapist, asked him to complete a fill-in-the-blank worksheet. She then asked him to answer comprehension questions related to a story. He was less than responsive, and at this point it was unclear to Ms. Rice if Devon understood the tasks or even understood how to use the device. Ms. Rice then tried simply conversing with Devon about current events (e.g., "What do you know about Hurricane Katrina?"), but his communication and general participation was also a struggle in that interaction. Finally, she decided to ask Devon about a topic she knew he loved: monster movies.

Devon particularly liked the movie *Young Frankenstein,* so Ms. Rice programmed information about the movie into the device and showed the young man how to hit the keys to share this information. He was prompted to walk around the school campus, find peers, and hit a key to ask the question, "Do you know the movie *Young Frankenstein*? Can I tell you about it?" When this content was used (and when his therapist gave him opportunities to interact in an authentic situations instead of only with her in her office), Devon immediately became more interested in communicating and began seeking out Ms. Rice to program new messages into his device. In addition, Devon's mother reported that he became interested in watching monster movies he had not seen before for the purpose of adding information about the films into his communication device.

Interests can also be used to increase communication opportunities and skills during lessons in the inclusive classroom. For instance, Zoe, a young woman with Asperger syndrome, was terrified of giving a speech in her communications class. When the teacher, Mr. Atkins, told his class that each student would have to deliver a persuasive political speech and learn new skills such as using repetition, smooth transitions, and parallel structure, Zoe became even more anxious. When Mr. Atkins realized how frazzled Zoe (and a few other students) had become, he told the entire class they could choose any topic for the first speech as long as they met the requirements. Zoe, who loves anything to do with South America, chose to deliver a persuasive speech encouraging classmates to visit the Amazon. Mr. Atkins videotaped this speech and gave Zoe detailed feedback on how to improve her skills. Zoe was then able to watch her tape several times (each time delighting in her own enthusiastic message about wildlife and rainforests) to learn new competencies and prepare for the next topic, which was not one of her choosing but was easier to approach with her newfound confidence.

ADDITIONAL IDEAS FOR EXPANDING COMMUNICATION SKILLS AND OPPORTUNITIES VIA INTERESTS OR PASSIONS

✦ As in Devon's story, use a student's fascination area as you introduce a new augmentative communication system. If you are trying to teach new sign language vocabulary, you might tie those words into a story featuring a favorite character or thing. If you are trying to introduce a new communication device, program language into the device that relates to the student's passion (e.g., fire, ladder, engine, Dalmatian) and consider adding phrases the student may find amusing or motivating (e.g., "Do you have any chandeliers in your house?"; "I love traffic lights!").

✦ When addressing skills related to syntax, morphology, and semantics, make the lesson more enjoyable by adding enthusiasms. One teacher we know had her second-grade student with autism practice making sentences by writing words on the backs of plastic pigs (one of the child's great loves) and allowing her to rearrange the figures into logical configurations. Another student was inspired to learn new vocabulary when his teacher asked him to define all of his weekly words by drawing a relevant scene, character, object, or event from the Harry Potter books (e.g., *aloft* was illustrated with a picture of kids playing Quidditch).

✦ Teach new language through a student's passion. Figurative language, which can confuse and frustrate many students with autism labels, might best be taught in the context of a student's "loves." A student who cannot grasp the meaning of the phrase "flying off the handle" might be able to learn it more easily if we give him several visual examples of his favorite character, Bugs Bunny, losing his cool after confrontations with Daffy Duck, Foghorn Leg Horn, and other members of the Warner Brothers gang.

4

To Help
Minimize Anxiety

*C*arey, a student with autism, often struggled in novel situations. If the school day was altered for the purpose of an assembly or if a substitute teacher showed up in his classroom, he often shrieked, paced, or crouched under his desk. Teachers tried everything from teaching relaxation techniques to reading Social Stories (Gray, 2003) to providing peer support and encouragement, but nothing seemed very effective. Then Carey's teacher, Ms. Sodenberg, came up with a strategy related to his area of fascination: James Bond films. When Carey was struggling, Ms. Sodenberg would tell him, "Change is good. James Bond changes from Sean Connery to Roger Moore to Timothy Dalton to Pierce Brosnan to Daniel Craig, and each one is as good, if not better, than the next!" Carey agreed with the statement but still had a hard time dealing with change in the moment. His teachers taught him a strategy of chanting all of the actors in the order they played Bond in order to bring his anxiety under control. The chant went something like this: "Change is okay. Something new can be just as good, if not better. Connery, Moore, Dalton, Brosnan, Craig." Other students in his class knew the chant, too, and would whisper it to Carey or with him in difficult moments.

Similarly, Mason, a middle school student with a love of cockroaches, struggled with social anxiety. He disliked the lunch room, the bus, parties, and any environment that was loud, unpredictable, and chaotic. He coped with this anxiety either by not entering these environments at all or by refusing to interact with others if he, somehow, did find himself in such places. All of this changed, fairly suddenly, when his teacher decided to use roaches to facilitate transitions into challenging spaces. Mr. Landry, his teacher, found at a novelty store a plastic roach that Mason could keep in his pocket at all times and wrote "I will survive" on the insect's back in permanent marker. He and Mason discussed how cockroaches have an unbelievable ability to survive, even in the most daunting conditions and circumstances. In fact, Mr. Landry told Mason, roaches are known for their ability to survive a nuclear blast! This lesson, combined with the introduction of the "pocket roach" (as we came to call it), made all the difference for Mason in social situations.

ADDITIONAL IDEAS FOR MINIMIZING ANXIETY VIA INTERESTS OR PASSIONS

★ If possible, point out, as Mr. Landry did, how the student's passion might be seen as a guide through tough times. This can be especially helpful if the student admires a certain person, animal, or character. For instance, if the child loves Dora the Explorer, you can point out how adventurous she is and how much she likes to try new things. Or if Martha Stewart is a "fave" (we have met more than one learner who loves the ultimate hostess), you might stress how this high-powered executive and homemaker extraordinaire has to gracefully change or adapt quickly when her recipe fails or when the weather unexpectedly freezes her newly planted annuals.

★ During times of challenge (e.g., transitions, novel situations), surround the student with images or reminders of his or her favorite things. Decorate the student's locker, notebook, or desk with these comforting images. Or create supports that can travel with the student, such as a comfort keychain or lucky charm that incorporates a favorite thing. Tip: To get images for these purposes, check magazines and Internet sites or even call companies related to the student's interests. One chain of gas stations sent a teacher three full boxes of materials when it learned she used its logo and products to help her student feel relaxed and comfortable in the classroom.

★ Teach the student to calm him- or herself by conjuring up thoughts of favorite things during tense times. You might even help the student construct a specific visualization consisting of a series of mental pictures that he or she can call on during frustrating times. At first, you may need to talk the student through the visualization so he or she can learn how to relax and move slowly through the images. For instance, Lawrence, a student who is a self-proclaimed "news nut" and fan of Katie Couric, could calm himself down by imagining himself reporting the nightly news alongside Katie and her colleagues.

5

To Plan for
Inclusive Schooling

Although all of the ideas in this book may help teachers provide more inclusive opportunities for students with autism and other disabilities, we want to offer a few thoughts on how to specifically use passions to accomplish this goal. Stewart, a student in a school where we both worked as educators, instantly comes to mind when we think of inclusion and interests. We learned that this third-grader loved the chef Emeril Lagasse. With this important knowledge in mind, we began planning for Stewart to enter an inclusive classroom for the first time in his schooling career. Because Stewart had attended a special education school for 4 years, all of the students in the classroom were new to him, the environment was new to him, and the daily activities were new to him. We knew we would need Emeril's help to comfort, motivate, reassure, teach, and support Stewart in this new experience. In the earliest stages of planning, we began thinking of various ways we could use Stewart's favorite person to increase his success in the new school. To begin with, we asked some peers to decorate the inside of Stewart's locker with pictures of Emeril (with dialogue bubbles coming out of the chef's mouth exclaiming "Welcome to Holmes School" and "Third grade is fun"). His desk was similarly adorned with small pictures of Emeril right next to a "cheat sheet" of cursive letters for Stewart's reference as he learned to write in this new style. Again, there was a dialogue bubble coming from Emeril's mouth; this one said, "Cursive writing is cool."

To start the year off right for Stewart, the homeroom teacher, Ms. Alvarez, decided to give a creative name to her daily schedule. In previous school years, Ms. Alvarez simply titled the list of hour-to-hour activities "Our Day"; this year, she called it "Today's Menu of Events." She also added a paper chef's hat to her collection of classroom props to use when she wanted to really motivate and energize Stewart and his classmates.

Finally, knowing how much her new student loved to make food (and that he had spent lot of time cooking in his life skills class at his previous special education school), Ms. Alvarez worked with the other third-grade teachers to develop a few lessons that would give the students in all three classes opportunities to learn through the creativity of the kitchen. For example, when the students studied the oceans and ocean life during a science unit, they worked with a visiting sushi chef to make sashimi. When they finished a unit on measurement, they celebrated by collaborating with the cafeteria staff to make a five-course meal that (of course) required them to measure using a variety of tools (e.g., measuring cups and spoons) and to use other math skills such as multiplication and division to determine portions and develop a grocery list.

Cole, another student we supported, loved OnStar, the in-vehicle security, communications, and diagnostics system designed and used by General Motors. Like Ms. Alvarez, Cole's teacher was sensitive to his needs and used his fascination to keep him comfortable in his inclusive classroom. Because Cole often pretended to phone OnStar when he needed help during class, his teacher decided to build him a booth that any student could use during choice time. Students who worked in the booth used the Internet and reference books to answer questions posed by their classmates. Cole, a map expert and a wiz at orienteering, delighted in working the OnStar booth and, more than any other task, loved giving students directions to one another's homes. His teacher also made him feel at home by using her "OnStar voice" when she really needed Cole's attention. By simply speaking in a robotic-sounding monotone, she found she could easily get Cole to follow directions and answer questions.

Additional Ideas for Planning for Inclusion via Interests or Passions

★ Consider launching a classroom theme related to a student's area of interest, as Ms. Alvarez did. If a learner loves roller coasters, for instance, desks can be "cars," assignments can be submitted at a "ticket window" (e.g., cardboard box labeled as such), and classroom rules might be played on a recording every week instead of simply being shared on a poster (e.g., "Attention members of Room 103, please keep in mind a few rules for your safety and comfort . . .).

★ Change the classroom environment or the student's personal space to reflect his or her fascination. Putting stickers on a student's desk or locker, creating a temporary bulletin board, or hanging posters that represent interests can be helpful.

★ Expand the instructional materials used in your classroom and explore if and how you might use supplies, supports, props, and even texts that reflect student passions. For instance, could writing tools (e.g., Mickey Mouse pencils), visual aids (e.g., Mickey Mouse "presenting" the water cycle), or math manipulatives (e.g., Mickey Mouse dominoes) motivate and inspire your learner?

6

To Build
Classroom Expertise

Students with autism often complain that they are reprimanded for talking about or otherwise sharing their interest area (Barron & Barron, 1992; Jackson, 2002; B. Moran, personal communication, November 9, 2005; Tammet, 2007). Imagine the possibilities for changing student attitudes and perspectives if students were invited not only to share their fascinations but also to serve as classroom experts and teachers in those areas.

For instance, a middle school teacher used an active learning technique called Match Game (Udvari-Solner & Kluth, in press) to showcase the talents of Marn, a young woman with autism who loved trains. During a unit on transportation and technology, Marn created one set of cards that contained concepts, words, and phrases related to trains. On the other set of cards, she wrote the corresponding definitions. One card, for instance, had the phrase, *run-through* written on it. The definition of *run-through* ("a train that generally is not scheduled to pick up or reduce railcars en route") was written on another card. Students had to find matches for terms and phrases that were, in most cases, completely new to them. Students had fun learning the new lingo and were impressed with Marn's expertise in this area. According to the teacher, the game was the first time students in her classroom had to go to Marn to *get* help and information. This experience changed students' perceptions of their classmate and gave Marn the courage to share more of her specialized knowledge with others. In addition, all students became interested in the activity and were anxious to take a turn designing their own set of cards for the group.

Another way teachers can give all students in their classrooms opportunities to serve as experts is by instituting activities or exercises that require students to share what they know, can do, and enjoy. One such approach that we and our colleagues have used is a classified advertisement activity. In this activity, all learners are asked to write an ad offering their services or expertise in a certain area (e.g., scrapbooking, organizing, math tutoring, telling jokes). Each student must also write a "help wanted" ad seeking assistance for any area in which he or she wants to gain skills or abilities (see Figure 1 for a sample advertisement and classified advertisement). Students might ask for or offer help in anything from designing origami to practicing math facts to learning to play tether-

Name: Reed S.

Help Wanted Ad	Classified Ad
I am looking for help with: • Finding after-school clubs • Learning to speak Spanish better • Learning slang	Please see me for help with: • Organizing your locker • Organizing your desk • Making reminder lists • Learning about North American reptiles • Making books about snakes

Figure 1. Sample student classified ad.

ball. Teachers instituting such a structure may be surprised by the diversity of student passions and the degree of interest learners have in educating and learning from one another. A seventh-grade teacher who used the classified ads model was astounded to learn that 9 of her 26 students signed up to learn lawnmower maintenance from a student with autism!

Finally, increasing student expertise might simply be a matter of finding moments for your students to shine and be recognized by peers. We fondly recall working with Matt, a middle school student who loved maps. Matt loved to draw, read, and interpret maps. When we visited him in his home, we saw some of his creations and were amazed at their detail and creativity. We were surprised, then, when we visited Matt's school and his teachers did not know much about his incredible abilities in mapmaking. We suggested that he be allowed to use his expertise in the classroom, and his teachers were only too happy to comply. They decided to display Matt's maps in the classroom and around the school and, when possible, to have Matt teach his peers map skills. During the first week of school alone, Matt taught both latitude and longitude and the concept of map scale to his peers.

ADDITIONAL IDEAS FOR BUILDING CLASSROOM EXPERTISE VIA INTERESTS OR PASSIONS

✦ Ask all learners about their strengths, loves, and fascinations. Some teachers do this with a whole-class discussion, whereas others do it by asking students to make a product to post in the classroom (e.g., a "Things I Can Do" or "My Interests" poster). Once those interests are posted or made public, remind students to use one another as resources.

✦ Provide ample opportunities for students to share their passions in the context of the curriculum or create team-building exercises that build on learners' areas of expertise. Whether you teach first grade or twelfth grade, regular community-building activities will strengthen student relationships and make it easier for learners to get and give support. Before you ask students to talk about Crazy Horse, suggest that they share their own personal heroes. As learners dive into an adventure story, ask them what elements would be part of their own adventure tale (e.g., ask "What objects would you bring? Which companions? Where would you go?") As students share this information over time, you will learn what students know and what they love and will be able to coach learners on how to depend upon one another.

✦ Structure specific opportunities to "advertise" the individual talents and fascinations of your students. Many teachers have a "student of the week" in the kindergarten year, but few carry this tradition into the upper grades. Having some way to highlight the accomplishments and uniqueness of each student during the year often makes it clear to teachers that all individuals have areas of expertise and interests that are special and out of the ordinary.

7

To Boost
Literacy Learning

*L*iane Holliday Willey (1999), a woman with Asperger syndrome, shared that her special interest in the American West during the 1800s led her to constantly read, explore, and learn in her childhood years. Willey rode her horse bareback (because that was how Native Americans rode), bought a cowboy hat with her first babysitting money, and inquired into her genealogy to see if she was related to the infamous gambler and gunfighter Doc Holliday. She also read, wrote, watched, and listened to materials related to her interest:

 When I was not watching the movies on television, looking through my vast collection of movie magazines or one of the dozens of books I had on the history of film, I was usually turning the pages of every fiction and non-fiction book I could find on cowboys and train robbers and American Indians and pioneers and western settlers. (p. 40)

Willey also shared that she wandered the archives of the library searching for books about Annie Oakley and Sitting Bull, made and repeatedly played audiotapes of television Westerns, and argued with her teachers when they encouraged her to focus on new topics (telling them it was her goal to read every book in the library on every western character she could find).

It is understandable why Willey's teachers would pester her to explore new topics. Educators typically want their students to use a wide range of materials and to explore a variety of texts as they learn to read and acquire new literacy skills. If students have certain fixations, however, teachers may want to allow these learners some freedom in choosing texts and pursuing related activities, as many individuals thrive academically when they can dive deeper into their special areas.

For example, we know one student, Jem, who, for weeks, only read books about rodents. Instead of spending a lot of time trying to pull him away from this interest area, Mr. Mueller, his teacher (who *did* want Jem to expand his reading selections eventually), chose to give Jem some time to conduct an in-depth investigation using any materials on rodents that he could find. For this 6-week period, Mr. Mueller did not hound Jem about adding new topics to his reading list and instead focused on other literacy objectives during this time. Although Jem did not learn much about new genres during this unit, Mr. Mueller worked with him on fluency, comprehension of informational texts, and acquisition of new vocabulary words. Furthermore, because Jem was granted permission to conduct an investigation, he became more comfortable in his classroom and with his teacher. In turn, when Mr. Mueller asked Jem to read *The Wind in the Willows* (Grahame, 1908), a fiction selection (albeit one with a rodent as a main character) for the next unit, Jem agreed.

We tried a similar technique with Trey, a student who did not speak, loved horses, and had a very active way of learning. Lesson planning was a real challenge because we had difficulty engaging Trey in typical classroom activities; he seemed uninterested in software programs, textbooks, workbooks, worksheets, learning games, and art supplies, preferring instead to play with a few horse figurines he kept in his backpack.

We thought we could persuade Trey to participate in classroom activities by buying him some horse magazines. We hoped that he might be able to look at them during breaks or after he finished classwork. When we showed the magazines to Trey, however, he was not interested in simply looking at them during breaks—he wanted to view them constantly! Trey would rummage through his desk to find the magazines the moment he came into the classroom and would pore through them during daily lessons. Although we were not getting him closer to the general education curriculum at this point, we realized that we had achieved at least a small victory: Trey was looking at literacy materials and he was sharing these materials with others. He also was tolerating our attempts to read him the stories that accompanied the wonderful photos.

Trey's teaching team, however, wanted to see if we could coax him into even more literacy routines and classroom exercises. The next step we took was to create classroom books using pictures from similar magazines. We made a social studies book from horse pictures (the topic was transportation, so we cut out pictures of horses pulling carts and people riding on horses). We made a reading book, too; taking vocabulary from class lessons, we created a short story about horses. We also pasted some of the photos into our basal reader and into other classroom favorites, adding a pony character to *Danny and the Dinosaur* (Hoff, 1992), *Stone Soup* (Brown, 1997), and even *Brrr! A Book About Polar Animals* (Berger & Berger, 2000). This last selection was fun for all of the students, as they never tired of giggling at the sight of a horse standing amid a colony of penguins. The adapted materials were a hit; Trey was able to stay with the class during lessons and could flip through his books if he needed to fidget. He was also able to learn new vocabulary and concepts by reading and rereading the much-loved horse books with teachers and classmates.

ADDITIONAL IDEAS
FOR BOOSTING LITERACY LEARNING
VIA INTERESTS OR PASSIONS

✦✦✦ Find a range of reading materials related to the student's fascination. Include in your search nonfiction, fiction, poetry, catalogs, pamphlets, and anything else that might pique the learner's interest. Keep in mind that some learners will be highly motivated to read materials that most of us do not find interesting or meaningful, such as telephone books, owner's manuals, cereal boxes, or junk mail flyers. One student we taught loved to read the fine print on the back of bank statements and credit card applications!

✦✦✦ Ask a student to write about his or her interest so that others may learn about it. Some students may even be able to write a children's book, technical manual, or comic book about their special area. Students can also be encouraged to write poems. Suggest that they try haiku, free verse, and even limericks using their "faves" as the topic area.

✦✦✦ Involve favorite characters or objects in the *act* of reading. One child we knew would participate in his literature circle only if he could take his turn reading aloud using an armadillo puppet. Another student who was a fan of Oprah Winfrey's television program gladly answered comprehension questions if we let him sit in the "Oprah set" we had constructed in the classroom. If he was interviewed (complete with inflatable microphone) he would not only answer the assigned questions, he would beg to be given more.

8

To Comfort

Teachers who understand the power of student passions as well as those who are simply concerned about making their students' lives as low stress as possible will explore how each learner's fascinations and areas of interest might be used in times of stress and difficulty. Too often, we face a student's crisis with warnings and consequences. Instead, we might provide access to a student's fascinations when times get tough. Not only does this strategy serve to make the student's day more relaxing but it also can make the teacher's day more calm and predictable as well!

Jimmy, a shy second-grader new to his school, was very uncomfortable any time there was a change or transition in his day. He remained most distressed when students were required to shift from one place in the classroom to another (e.g., moving from their desks to the reading corner). After 2 difficult weeks, Ms. Richards, the general education teacher, decided to give her room a makeover that her young student could not resist. Because Jimmy loved the Chihuahua featured in the Taco Bell ads, Ms. Richards decided to make the dog a part of the classroom. She went to the local branch of the fast-food restaurant and asked staff if they had any placemats she could have. Ms. Richards used the placements to show Jimmy where to sit at his reading table and where to sit on the group-time rug. She also got him a little stuffed-toy Chihuahua to carry around when he was feeling nervous or in need of support.

Another teacher, Ms. Cooney, was aware that her student, Mary Chris, frequently had difficulty (including screaming, biting herself, and occasionally biting others) during fire drills. Ms. Cooney used this student's passion to keep her focused and relaxed during these stressful times. Usually the principal would tell Mary Chris that the drill was coming so she could prepare somewhat. Once the word came down from the office, Ms. Cooney would let Mary Chris listen to her Patsy Cline CDs until the drill began (a special treat that always calmed Mary Chris down). When the alarm sounded, Ms. Cooney would pull Mary Chris to the front of the line and softly sing "Walking After Midnight" as the students marched to their designated emergency spot. This was all the support the young girl needed; with this sensitive strategy in place, Mary Chris would quietly and quickly walk out of the building beside her teacher.

These stories show that Ms. Richards and Ms. Cooney understand how, for some students, passions provide a sense of security, confidence, and even companionship.

Most of us understand the importance of a teddy bear to a small child but think less about how favorite items and ideas bring solace to grown adults (and not just to those on the autism spectrum). We have a friend who always watches *Gone with the Wind* when she is feeling low and another pal who keeps a "lucky" owl figurine with him at all times but especially when he travels on a plane, as he is terrified of flying. We might be able to offer more sensitive supports to our students if we can reflect on how often we too use our preferences as comforts.

ADDITIONAL IDEAS
FOR COMFORTING STUDENTS
VIA INTERESTS OR PASSIONS

✦ Allow the student to spend time with his or her "faves" during times of distress or difficulty. You might even provide a comfort space somewhere in the school where the learner can go to relax and "visit" preferred materials or activities. One teacher we know allowed her student with autism to keep a miniature penguin collection in a drawer in the back of the classroom. The drawer could be visited in case of emotional emergencies.

✦ Remind staff to turn to the student's fascinations during times of difficulty. If the student is upset or having a "meltdown," it may help to remind him or her of favorite things by chanting or singing about them, by showing photos of them, or simply by reminding the student to focus on or daydream about his or her special areas of interest.

✦ It is often helpful to include a student's fascinations or areas of expertise a part of a behavior plan. Consider all of the ways a learner's special interests might be used to *prevent* difficulty and keep students calm. Specifically, look for ways to infuse favorite materials and activities throughout the student's day.

9

To Inspire
Career Ideas

Think back to when you were a student. You took a variety of required subjects and at one point in high school, you were expected to move more toward your interests for the purpose of exploring careers. People with autism, of course, deserve the same freedom and right to this tradition. Passions can give direction for following one's heart to a career path.

For instance, Eric was very passionate about fire trucks. Whenever he saw one, he grinned broadly, laughed excitedly, and took measures to view the fire truck for as long as possible (which occasionally meant that he would run for blocks). An insightful teacher, aware of the joy that fire trucks brought to Eric's day, arranged an apprenticeship for him. Eric was given high school credit to volunteer at the firehouse as part of the school's service-learning curriculum. He was responsible for tasks such as hosing off the trucks, cleaning the floors, and helping with food preparation (including the five-alarm chili for which this firehouse was known). Eric's co-workers viewed him as helpful and calm and valued his commitment to order, safety, and cleanliness (all critical in a firehouse).

Linking interests to careers is exactly what Temple Grandin, a woman with autism, suggests. Grandin (1995), who is a very successful designer of livestock equipment, credits her science teacher Mr. Carlock with inspiring her to pursue her career and her area of research. Grandin shares that this creative teacher used her interest in cattle chutes to motivate her to study both psychology and science. Today, Grandin travels all over the country and the world designing stockyards and chutes for major meat-packing firms. She is a recognized leader in her field and has authored dozens of technical and scientific papers on livestock handling.

Another author of a popular autobiography, Dawn Prince-Hughes (2004), followed her passion of gorillas from adolescence into adulthood and found that her interest could serve her not only personally (she often found visits to the zoo soothing and inspiring) but professionally as well. Because Prince-Hughes has such an uncanny knack for understanding the behavior, emotions, and relationships of these animals, she thrived in a program that allowed her to study the creatures and teach others about them. Today, she is an anthropologist, primatologist, ethnologist, and a college professor specializing in—what else—primates!

Additional Ideas for Inspiring Career Ideas via Interests or Passions

✦✦✦ Assign students the task of studying occupations related to their area of interest. For instance, hundreds of jobs might be explored if a learner loves computers, including software developer, engineer, information systems manager, statistician, game tester, salesperson, administrative assistant, web designer, and even movie editor. This is a useful exercise no matter how obscure or unusual the interest area might be, as students will find that there are related careers for most passions. After all, there may not be hundreds (or even dozens) of jobs related to cannons, but there are certainly a few, including working in a museum, performing in Civil War reenactments, and conserving and repairing artillery. See Table 1 for a list one team generated for a student who was crazy about pets, especially dogs. Creating such a list can be a helpful way to start a conversation about a student's future vocational goals.

Table 1. Careers and jobs related to dogs

Animal behaviorist
Animal control officer
Animal shelter staff
Boarding kennel worker
Creator of novelty items (e.g., homemade dog treats, toys, pet-related gift items) to sell online or in a specialty store
Dog exerciser
Dog food and pet accessories shop worker
Dog show handler
Dog show judge
Dog show superintendent
Dog sitter
Dog trainer
Dog walker
Groomer
Guide dog trainer
Member of police or military K-9 unit

Table 1. *(continued)*

Professional field trialer (i.e., train dogs for field trials)
Receptionist in a veterinarian's office
Staff member at a pet- or dog-related organization (e.g., American Kennel Club,
    People for the Ethical Treatment of Animals)
Veterinarian
Veterinary researcher
Veterinary technician/assistant
Writer (e.g., for a dog magazine)

✦ If your curriculum permits it, bring people into the classroom from various career paths. Include those who represent common choices (e.g., police officer) and those who might be farther off the beaten path (e.g., entomologist), especially if these options match student interests. You might even ask these guests to talk about how their childhood and adolescent fascinations helped them choose their career paths.

✦ Use a student's passions as a tool during transition planning. From the middle school years on, keep the learner's abilities, strengths, and favorites central as supports are created, plans are crafted, and dreams are imagined.

10

To Encourage
Risk Taking

At times, life passages may involve certain risks. Think back to when you were learning to ride a bicycle. Remember that day when your parents took off the training wheels and let go? Were you afraid to fall? Maybe you did fall on your first try. Your parents took a risk by letting go because there is dignity in being able to ride a bike.

Sometimes opportunities are taken away from a student with autism under the guise of safety or simply because the individual has a disability. This can result in subtle to very blatant discrimination. For example, Fernando, a student living in the Chicago area, was passionate (to say the least) about basketball. He had basketball posters all over his room and basketball cards jammed in his desk at school, he wore jerseys and sports-related T shirts almost daily, and he played basketball at the park as often as possible. His favorite team was the Chicago Bulls, and his favorite player was Michael Jordan.

The summer following Fernando's fifth-grade year, he applied to and was invited to attend Michael Jordan basketball camp. One member of the school community was doubtful about Fernando's ability to participate and asked questions such as, "What will Fernando do there?" "Will he be safe with all of the competitive players?" and "Would he be better off at a disability-focused camp?" Fernando's mother, however, did not dwell on these areas of negativity or doubt. Instead, she decided to embrace the dignity of risk.

As a result, Fernando had the experience of a lifetime due not only to the positive attitudes of many people in his life (especially his mother) but also to his love of basketball. He was thrilled about attending the prestigious camp and participated in all of the drills and exercises. His basketball skills improved, he got to meet Michael Jordan, and he even had his picture taken with his hero. Sure, there were risks associated with attending this camp, as there are for most of the good things in life, but this camp allowed Fernando to live his passion, and surely that achievement is worth a little uncertainty.

Another mother learned this same lesson when her sons' fascination inspired both learning and risk taking. Karla, the mother of twin boys with autism, initially lamented their new focus on frogs. The biggest concern for this mother of active boys was frog-catching equity. When one of her boys caught a frog and the other did not, there were sometimes tears and disappointment. Karla's frustration with this competition ended, however, when she suddenly realized her sons were touching frogs! As Karla explained

in her online blog about being a homeschooling mom (http://www.homeschoolblogger.
com/karlakayakins): "These are the little boys that couldn't even touch a wash cloth
before—and now they are touching toads and frogs! Not only touching them but catch-
ing them!" In addition to helping these youngsters take "tactile risks," this new fascination inspired family-wide learning. Karla shared, "It's really amazing! So far we have found
the common toad, and a green frog and a wood frog. Toads, frogs, slugs, crickets—they
are all a part of the collection of critters the boys are enjoying."

When working with students with autism, it is important to remember that although
safety, protection, and predictability are important, so are novelty and adventure. When
considering new a experience for a student—whether it is a new schooling choice (e.g., an
inclusive classroom), a new social endeavor (e.g., dating for the first time), or a new community or recreation opportunity (e.g., joining a sports team)—it will serve teachers well to
consider how student interests might be used to facilitate the experience.

ADDITIONAL IDEAS
FOR ENCOURAGING RISK TAKING
VIA INTERESTS OR PASSIONS

✦ Use a passion-inspired activity or event to coax a student into new behaviors or experiences. A student who is reluctant to ask directions in a typical situation might be inspired to do so on the class field trip to the Air and Space Museum if he knows those directions lead him to a Tomcat fighter jet exhibit.

✦ Consider different risk-taking moments that students are likely to face in your classroom or during the school year (e.g., giving a speech in front of the class, inviting a friend to play at recess) and, in advance, brainstorm ways these risks can be either minimized or made palatable to the student by connecting his or her area of interest.

✦ For a student who nearly always needs a nudge to try new things or to wander into the realm of the unknown, try keeping a grab bag of inspiration that the student can use to experience something new. The bag might include a few favorite things related to the learner's passion (e.g., charms, toys, special objects), a few words of encouragement on an index card (e.g., "Go for it!", "You can do it!"), and maybe a short story about past successes the student had after taking a risk. We got this idea from Lee, a student who was passionate about travel trailers. Lee had such a bag that was kept in his teacher's desk and could be used during any risk-taking situation. He used it during the school spelling bee and before he had to make an announcement to the student body. The bag contained a polished stone with the word *try* on it, a favorite pop-up camper keychain, and several magazine photos of RVs.

To Connect Students to Standards-Based Content

$\mathcal{W}$e have worked with students interested in Korea, vacuum cleaners, screwdrivers, fences, chickens, James Bond, stop signs, churches, weathervanes, triangles, remote controls, dragons, and basketball. Any of these interests, no matter how obscure or unusual, can be used as part of a standards-based curriculum. For example, one student, Freddie, loved to "do the calendar." Part of the reason why this was so central to his life was that he had spent 6 years in a self-contained classroom where students of all ages engaged in a calendar exercise daily. Therefore, when we started working with Freddie, his favorite activity was studying the months of the year and answering questions about the holidays and special events (e.g., Independence Day, Christmas, First Day of Spring).

Although this interest in the calendar was not hurting Freddie's education, it also was not helping him to grow as a learner. To enhance Freddie's learning and to challenge all students in his sixth-grade classroom, we developed a calendar activity appropriate for older students. All of the students in the classroom knew the days of the week and the months of the year, but none of them knew that December 7 was the anniversary of the bombing of Pearl Harbor or that the date of the spring equinox can change from year to year. The teachers had all of the students work in small groups to find important dates related to history, science, literature, and math. Freddie was responsible for presenting the event-of-the-day each morning. All students—including Freddie—learned something new, and Freddie was thrilled to have a calendar activity incorporated into the daily schedule.

In addition to tapping into a learner's knowledge base, teachers might also target special skill areas. In a study of inclusive classrooms by Kasa-Hendrickson and Kluth (2005), a teacher, Ms. Holder, used one of her student's areas of prowess as a tool for connecting her to standards-based social studies learning:

 I want her to realize that she is very good at doing some things on her own. So I asked myself, "What is Shantel good at on her own?" Puzzles. She is great at puzzles. I knew another teacher had this magnetic puzzle globe so I asked if I could borrow it. Shantel needs to learn about Europe. It is important for her to have the same academic experiences and I might as well incorporate what she is good at to do it. (p. 9)

Not only was Ms. Holder able to find classroom time for Shantel to work on the puzzles she so loved but she also found a creative way to push her student into complex content by using a skill that the learner prized.

The instructional decision made by Ms. Holder might be applauded by Temple Grandin (2006), a woman with autism who wished that her teachers would have understood the connections that could have been drawn between fixations and academic content. One of Grandin's fascinations as a teenager was sliding doors and, as an adult, she explained how this interest might have been exploited to improve her education: "If my teacher had challenged me to learn how the electronic box that opened the door worked, I would have dived head first into electronics. Fixations can be tremendous motivators" (p. 2). She went on to share that teachers should use fixations to motivate instead of trying to stamp them out. Grandin's sentiment is similar to one that we often share with teachers: "Don't squash interests, exploit them!"

ADDITIONAL IDEAS FOR CONNECTING STUDENTS TO STANDARDS-BASED CONTENT VIA INTERESTS OR PASSIONS

⋆ ⋆ ⋆ Search the curriculum for natural areas to teach about the student's favorites. If the student loves vacuum cleaners, this topic can be quite easily featured in a unit on inventions. If the student adores dolphins, you can discuss them during lessons on habitats or ocean life. And if the student values Sherlock Holmes, this topic can be explored not only during reading or English classes but also during studies about deduction, problem solving, or literary genres.

⋆ ⋆ ⋆ Look at the standards for the learner's grade level and determine how you can adapt them to a student's needs by using his or her passion. For instance, we know a U.S. history teacher who taught the standard "Explain the United States' relationship to other nations and its role in international organizations" by using an analogy of the Super Friends cartoon characters. This learner was able to understand and even explain the role of the United States in the United Nations after he was shown a visual aid comparing this relationship to the one that Aquaman, the Wonder Twins, and Superman have with the Justice League. Consider ways in which any standard might seem less abstract and complex by using such comparisons.

⋆ ⋆ ⋆ Consider how you can change your instruction to meet the needs of students with specific and significant areas of expertise. Can you comically imitate a favorite person, place, or thing when trying to emphasize a point or give directions? Can you use the students' interests in your lectures or whole-class discussions (e.g., "A car and a CRH 5 bullet train started from the two different towns at the same time . . .")?

12

To Encourage
In-Depth Study

Projects are an ideal learning activity for those students with autism who need some time alone to work independently and those who thrive when given opportunities to immerse themselves in one topic. Many students are thrilled to explore their fascinations in detail, not only to succeed academically but also to satisfy personal curiosity. Donna Williams (1992), a woman with autism, found that she could be academically successful when a favorite teacher believed in her abilities and let her pursue a topic of special interest in depth:

 While the other teachers found me a devil, this teacher found me to be bright, amusing, and a pleasure to teach. At the end of the term, I handed her the most important piece of schoolwork any of my high school teachers had received.

The students had all been given a set date and topic on which to write. I had been intrigued by the way black people had been treated in America in the sixties.

I told my teacher that what I wanted to do was a secret, and she agreed to extend my due date as I enthusiastically informed her of the growing length of my project. I had gone through every book I could find on the topic, cutting out pictures and drawing illustrations over my written pages, as I had always done, to capture the feel of what I wanted to write about. The other students had given her projects spanning an average of about three pages in length. I proudly gave her my special project of twenty-six pages, illustrations, and drawings. She gave me an A. (p. 81)

And Daniel Tammet (2007), a man with autism, shared in his autobiography, *Born on a Blue Day,* how elated he was to be given the task of compiling a report on the Summer Olympics:

 [After getting the assignment,] I spent the next week cutting and gluing hundreds of photos of the athletes and events from newspapers and magazines onto colored cardboard sheets, my father helping me with the scissors. The choice of how to organize the different cuttings was made by a logic that was entirely visual: athletes dressed in red were pasted onto one sheet, those in yellow were put on another, those in white on a third, and so on. On smaller sheets of lined paper I wrote out in my best handwriting a long list of the names of all the countries I found mentioned in the newspapers with participants in the games. I also wrote a list of all the different events, including tae kwon do—Korea's national sport—and table tennis, which made its Olympic debut in Seoul. There were also lists of statistics and scores, including event points, race times, records broken and medals won. In the end, there were so many sheets of cuttings and written pages that my father had to hole-punch each one and tie them together with string. On the front cover I drew a picture of the Olympic rings in their colors of blue, yellow, black, green and red. My teacher gave me top marks for the amount of time and effort I had put into the project. (p. 63)

Teachers may balk at allowing students to complete projects based on their passion, but many learners show us their best work when allowed to focus on a fascination area. A teacher in this situation who is leery of "giving in" to a student's favorite topic yet again might feel better about this decision if he or she can focus on teaching the student related skills (e.g., reading, writing, organization, interviewing, notetaking) as part of the project or on pushing the student into new areas of content as he or she explores a passion area. If the child likes spiders, for instance, and knows a lot about different species, habits, and characteristics, the teacher might insist that the student add a map of the world and highlight which types of spiders can be found in different countries to be sure that geography is being learned as well as spider facts. Or if the student has already completed a lot of work related to his or her area of interest, he or she might be encouraged to study a related topic. For instance, when one young man wanted to do a science fair project on robots for the third year in a row, his father finally convinced him to explore technology used by people with disabilities (including robotic limbs).

ADDITIONAL IDEAS FOR ENCOURAGING IN-DEPTH STUDY VIA INTERESTS OR PASSIONS

✶ Consider all of the skills and competencies that can be addressed and encouraged as part of project-based instruction. Literacy skills such as reading, writing, speaking, and listening can be taught or assessed. Study skills including research, notetaking, and outlining can be honed. Students might also be introduced to new technology through projects, including word processing, PowerPoint, and the use of assistive technology. Students can also practice communication and social skills through in-depth study if the work is structured to give students these opportunities.

✶ Allow students to conduct ongoing (perhaps even multiyear) projects of their favorite people, topics, or things. You might encourage these learners to keep a portfolio, binder, or crate in the classroom that houses all of their accumulated products, artifacts, and materials. When opportunities for new projects arise, a student can then reference his or her accumulated materials and be encouraged to examine a new question related to the area of fascination.

✶ Have students keep a running list of questions related to their passion area. In particular, you might ask learners to generate "big" questions that can lead them to study their passions in real-world or authentic ways. For instance, instead of having students study national parks and complete basic research on them (e.g., what they are, where they are located), you might push them to use their projects to answer real and perhaps provocative or investigative questions without "right" answers, such as, "Are national parks endangered?" or "What is the purpose of a national park?" or "How have the purposes of national parks evolved?"

13

To Make Sense of a Confusing World

Individuals with autism often report that the "neurotypical" world is confusing and difficult to negotiate at times. Students may struggle to read social situations, to figure out communication norms, or to learn rules, expectations, and etiquette. One way that some learners cope with this confusion is to turn to their passions to find refuge and to make order from disorder. For example, in his book *A Different Kind of Boy*, Daniel Mont (2001) recalled that his son, Alex, immersed himself in board games to find certainty and parameters:

 The world is a confusing and overwhelming place but the rules of a board game are well defined. You know when it is your turn. You know exactly what to do. You can sit back and enjoy the surprises and random events because the outcomes are bounded. Alex was never as at ease as when he played his games. (p. 56)

Sean Barron, a man with autism and coauthor of *There's a Boy in Here* (Barron & Barron, 1992), also used fascinations as a way to create order and peace. His passion for dead-end streets helped him cope with the constant swirl of information, expectations, stimuli, and demands. When he saw dead-end streets, however, he felt relief and he knew with certainty that the road stopped. With this piece of information, Sean could put his energy into how the road would end. He would wonder if it might be a cul-de-sac, a wall, a fence, or another type of barrier. With these thoughts running through his mind, Sean could relax and face challenges and uncertainty because in this part of his world at least, there was order and predictability.

Similarly, a young man we know, Blake, uses his love of tools to make sense of things around him. Blake's favorite show is the PBS program *New Yankee Workshop*, which features do-it-yourself projects and interviews with talented craftsmen. By watching this program and by studying tools on his own, he has become an expert in the history, brands, and types of various power and woodworking tools. This fixation has given him an interesting pastime and made his life richer in general; however, in at least one instance, it also helped him to decipher the chaotic world of sports. During a Friday night high school football game in his hometown, the Grizzlies (wearing blue and gold) were playing the Eagles (wearing green and yellow). Throughout the first half of the game, Blake's mom, Shelly, pointed out players and explained plays to Blake. Despite Shelly's best efforts, however, Blake showed little interest in the game. Suddenly, Blake gave the field a second look. A smile of relief came to his face as he pointed to the teams and said, "Wood Tech versus Delta." (Wood Tech is a tool company whose primarily colors are green and yellow, and Delta tools are blue and silver.) Due to the connection between tools and football, Blake remained engaged in the football game for longer time than his parents expected that evening. For once, he attempted to understand the jumble of downs, goals, and touchdowns and was able to enjoy the game.

ADDITIONAL IDEAS FOR MAKING SENSE OF A CONFUSING WORLD VIA INTERESTS OR PASSIONS

⋆⭑⋆ Look for metaphors that might work in a given situation, as Blake did at the football game. A dreaded field trip might be viewed as a safari for a child who loves jungle life, and a trip to the school nurse could be described as preventative maintenance or a pit stop for a youngster who follows NASCAR.

⋆⭑⋆ Follow students' leads to learn more about their needs and how they use their passions in this capacity. If you watch learners with autism or Asperger syndrome during challenging moments, you may see them arranging favorite figurines or immersing themselves in a favorite book. Point out this tendency to those working with such students so they will see this behavior as purposeful and necessary.

⋆⭑⋆ Teach students to go to their passions in moments of confusion. When students seem to crave order or understanding, you can suggest that they use their favorites to decode the situation or event. You can do this by asking them if they want or need preferred materials, objects, or activities or by seeing if they can make a comparison between the perceived chaos and their area of interest (e.g., "What would Bob the Builder do now?", "How is going on to middle school like Charles Lindbergh's flight across the Atlantic?")

14

To Let Students Shine and Showcase Talents

Students with autism may want to use their passion or fascination to show off their talents and demonstrate to others that they are intelligent. This may be especially important for learners who have been seen or labeled as challenging or difficult. Sean Barron, for instance, recalls that he relished opportunities to dazzle others with his knowledge of radio and television call letters:

 I knew it was knowledge that few other people had, and that made me feel excited and powerful—so much so that I kept a list of the call letters in my head. On any given day one station's letters would stick in my head, repeating themselves over and over. I'd use these repeating letters to shut out the people around me and all the things going on that I didn't like. The sound of the letters was strong and vivid, blotting out all my insecurities. I did this for many years and it always made me feel powerful. I was the only one in the entire school who had this information, and as long as the letters spoke in my head, I was no longer inferior. (Barron & Barron, 1992, p. 120)

Of course if an individual talks too much or too long about his or her special interest, that person can run the risk of being viewed as rude, boring, or self-centered (Klin, Carter, & Sparrow, 1997). For this reason, students are often told not to carry on about their fascinations and to avoid long monologues related to their passions. We disagree with this advice, as many students with autism have too few opportunities to shine. Instead, we promote teaching students how to monitor their conversations and how to share what they know in sensitive and appropriate ways. If possible, look for natural opportunities for learners to show their smarts. Speech class or the debate team might be a vehicle for those who want structured ways to share what they know. Clubs are another possibility. A student who loves to solve problems might want to join the math decathlon, and a learner who is crazy about animals might find plenty of opportunities to share his or her knowledge in 4-H meetings.

ADDITIONAL IDEAS FOR LETTING STUDENTS SHINE AND SHOWCASING TALENTS VIA INTERESTS OR PASSIONS

✦✦✦ Be sure to give all students opportunities to demonstrate what they know. Consider, perhaps, planning a "tell us what you know" talent show that focuses on all students' areas of expertise. Students can choose to give a short presentation on their areas of special interest or to simply stand before the group and field questions from classmates.

✦✦✦ Help students create a résumé, portfolio, or scrapbook so they can showcase special talents or areas of expertise in a formal way. This exercise serves two purposes. Perhaps the most important function is to show students a way to organize their accomplishments or special skills. Even if a student's interest is a bit unusual, such as kitchen whisks, having the responsibility of putting everything in one place and arranging it for others to see can give the learner a feeling of pride and accomplishment, as well as practice in organizing, categorizing, and in displaying information in an attractive and logical way (e.g., recipes that require whisks, ideas for using different types of whisks). The second purpose is to teach students related skills such as how to prioritize information or experiences or how to write in a compelling fashion.

✦✦✦ Introduce students to the theory of multiple intelligences (Gardner, 1993) and specifically to the work of Thomas Armstrong, author of *You're Smarter Than You Think: A Kid's Guide to Multiple Intelligences* (2002). This text is written for students and is designed to inspire them to stop asking *if* they are smart and begin asking *how* they are smart. Students on the spectrum may be interested in having new ways to discuss their intelligence and ability.

"To Give Students "Power"

The Power Cards strategy, developed by Elisa Gagnon (2001), is another way to use a student's special interest as a tool for support. The technique consists of 1) a story about a strategy that a student's hero has used to solve a problem, which is usually written on a single page, and 2) the Power Card itself, which is the size of a business card and recaps how the person using the card can use the same strategy to solve a similar problem. The Power Card Strategy can be used in a variety of situations, including when an individual is confused about the requirements or rules of a situation, does not understand choices, is struggling with generalizations, needs visual supports to act, or needs help to remember what to do in a specific situation.

For instance, in her book *Power Cards,* Gagnon (2001) shared a story about Kimberly, a young woman with autism who usually hugs people when she greets them. Because Kimberly is getting older and meeting a wider range of people, her family wants her to learn to shake hands when she meets new people. Kimberly loves Shania Twain, so a story about the popular entertainer was written for her. In this story, Shania learns that it isn't always best to hug everyone. She decides to shake hands with her many fans instead of hugging them (especially those she is meeting for the first time). At the end of the story, Shania shares three tips with the reader:

1. Smile and put out your right hand and shake the other person's right hand.
2. Introduce yourself and ask the person how they are.
3. Practice greetings with your friends and teachers. (p. 43)

Kimberly's Power Card featured a photo of Shania Twain and these three tips. Kimberly could review both the story and the card repeatedly and carry the card with her for those times when she might be meeting a lot of new people. Figure 2 shows how the Power Card Strategy was used to help a student become less dependent on prompts.

Wilbur Takes Charge
by Cindy Van Horn

Charlotte the spider loves her best friend, Wilbur the pig. Lately, Charlotte has been frustrated with Wilbur because he will not do anything unless she tells him what to do. Wilbur will not eat unless Charlotte tells him it is time to eat. Wilbur will not clean his pigpen unless Charlotte tells him to clean it. In fact, Wilbur won't even play with the other pigs unless Charlotte tells him it's time to play. Charlotte is tired! She knows Wilbur will be a happier pig if he asks for help instead of always having to be told what to do.

Just like Wilbur, it is important for all boys at school to be independent. It is important to do your work on your own without someone telling you what to do. If you don't know what to do, it is OK to ask for help. For example, boys can go through the lunch line by themselves without someone telling them every step they need to take. Of course, boys can always ask for help if they need it. Charlotte has decided she is going to wait for Wilbur to ask for help instead of always telling him what to do. She wants Wilbur to take charge!

Just remember Charlotte's three rules for taking charge:

1. If you are not sure what to do, check your schedule.

2. Don't wait for someone to tell you what to do. Just do it!!

3. If you need help say, "I need help."

   Remember these three things and you can take charge just like Wilbur!

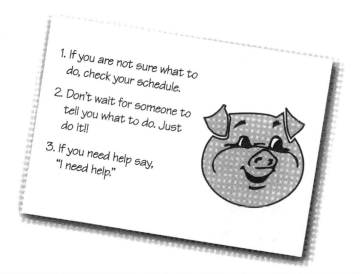

Figure 2. Example Power Card Strategy involving characters from a student's favorite videotape (*Charlotte's Web*) to help the student become less dependent on prompts. (From Gagnon, E. [2001]. *Power Cards: Using special interests to motivate children and youth with Asperger syndrome* [pp. 48–49]. Shawnee Mission, KS: Autism Asperger Publishing Company [http://www.asperger.net]; reprinted by permission.)

Additional Ideas for Giving Students "Power" via Interests or Passions

★ Allow all students (those with and without disability labels) to make Power Cards for themselves. Ask students to think of situations, experiences, and events that make them uncomfortable or nervous. Then ask them to think of one of their passions or areas of special interest. Teach them how to integrate these things into a story and then into a Power Card that they can keep in their locker, wallet, or desk.

★ If the Power Card strategy is particularly effective for one of your students, you might consider additional ways to keep the "1, 2, 3 information" handy for that individual. For instance, the same information that appears on a Power Card can be posted inside a locker or desk. It can be slipped into the front see-through cover of a binder or into an acrylic keychain picture frame. It even can be made into a set of stickers (printed from a computer onto mailing labels) that can be applied to any number of materials or surfaces.

★ Although most of the examples provided thus far have been related to encouraging certain behaviors, Power Cards can also be used to help students sharpen study skills and learn new academic content. For instance, a card could be developed to remind students of grammar rules or of how to use a protractor.

16

To Encourage Chit-Chat

Students with autism, particularly those with Asperger syndrome and others who have reliable communication, are often accused of having poor social skills and, specifically, of being unable to engage in small talk successfully. Students may struggle with this skill because they have a hard time figuring out how to enter a conversation or simply because they may not feel comfortable participating in a conversation that does not pertain to subjects they know well. Encouraging students to join conversations by chatting about their favorites is one way to ease fears, anxieties, and doubts in this area.

Of course it can be a problem if the student only talks about his or her passions when engaged in small talk, but we feel that if the learner is taught to monitor things like how long he or she is talking about the passion or if he or she has created spaces for turn-taking in the conversation, fascinations can be a perfectly appropriate topic for chit-chat with acquaintances and strangers alike. This is important considering that if the student does not use his or her area of expertise as a way into the conversation, he or she may not enter it at all.

Another reason to encourage the student's interests as part of his or her conversation toolbox is that many learners demonstrate better communication skills when they are speaking about their fascinations. Winter-Messiers (2007) found that the individuals with autism in her study changed fairly dramatically when they were invited to chat about their special interests. She noticed, for instance, that the intelligibility of the participants increased markedly, as did the sophistication of their use of vocabulary, word order, and syntax:

 For example when responding to general questions, Charlie repeatedly gave answers such as "Uh, I don't think so, just whatever," consisting of simple one- or two-syllable words with no clear content or syntax. When asked about his favorite thing to play with, however, his speech pattern changed instantly as he confidently replied, "My favorite is a Yu-Gi Oh! Card that combines with three Blue-Eyed White Dragons, and due to polymerization it forms those three into a three-headed dragon." (p. 147)

The researcher and her team also documented improvement in body language and a decrease in distraction and repetitive behaviors when students discussed their fascinations.

ADDITIONAL IDEAS
FOR ENCOURAGING CHIT-CHAT
VIA INTERESTS OR PASSIONS

⋆✦⁺ Give students structured time in the classroom to simply make small talk. This might be the first 5 or 10 minutes of the day on Friday mornings or at the end of a class period when you have finished wrapping up the lesson. You can remind students with autism that they can use their areas of fascination to start conversations. Remind them also to give others opportunities to choose topics and share *their* areas of interest.

⋆✦⁺ Create opportunities for students to formally learn about and use conversation skills—for instance, by using a collaborative structure called Dinner Party (Udvari-Solner & Kluth, in press). In this activity, students begin by moving randomly around the classroom until they hear the teacher shout out a number. They then form groups based on that number. If 4 is called, for instance, students immediately find the students nearest to them and form a group. The teacher then gives an open-ended question (e.g., "How do you reduce stress when taking a test?", "What do you know about poetry?") that the students discuss within their groups until the teacher indicates that time is up. At this point, students begin wandering around the classroom once again and wait for another number to be called and topic to be introduced. This structure could be used to give several different students in the classroom opportunities to showcase their interests. The teacher can either structure opportunities for specific students to shine by naming different student interests during the activity (e.g., "Share what you know about plumbing" followed by "Share what you know about motorcycle racing") or ask students to individually share about their favorites (e.g., "Share something about an area of expertise you have").

⋆✦⁺ When teaching new conversation skills, try using a student's area of interest to engage him or her. Have a conversation about barbecue grills, for instance, and ask the student to practice turn taking or asking relevant questions. If the student has a speech therapist, involve him or her in this activity.

To Boost Mathematics Skills and Competencies

It is not uncommon for students with autism to have a love of or skill with numbers and mathematics. One teen recalls how his passion for using numbers and making calculations began when, as a boy of 3, he noticed a calendar with "large black and red figures" (Bosch, as cited in Attwood, 1998, p. 119) hanging in the baker's shop in his village:

 I soon discovered that such shapes were also to be found on doors of houses, on pages of books, and in newspapers. Suddenly my tiny world consisted of nothing but numbers, much to my parents' worry . . . I knew clearly what it meant to be three years old: one had been in the world for 1, 2, 3 years. Then I proceeded, quite unaided, from counting to 'arithmetic'. When I was four, so I am told, I announced triumphantly to my mother, 'Even if you won't tell me, I know how much 4 times 25 is. It's 100 because 2 times 50 is also 100'. (Bosch, as cited in Attwood, 1998, p. 119)

Although such stories are fascinating and have become part of the "folklore" of autism, not all learners on the spectrum are "human calculators" or even capable and comfortable with numbers. For example, Tova, a young woman with the label of pervasive developmental disorder (PDD), often struggled in her math classes until her teacher used her area of special interest to draw her into classwork. Tova, a fan of competitive swimming and diving, was always more willing to engage in the daily lesson if the teacher mentioned her favorite sports. Fractions lessons were enhanced by discussions of how many lanes of the pool were filled with swimmers from a certain team or how much of a race a swimmer had completed when he or she had finished a certain number of laps. Tova especially loved her teacher to challenge her with fun swim-related extra-credit problems such as "What is the area of one lane of the swimming pool?" or "Including all events, how much distance did a certain athlete swim during a meet?"

Similarly, Myles (2005) recounted how teachers supported Khalid, a boy with Asperger syndrome, in his love of tornadoes. For instance, his math teacher developed activities that required him to figure out things such as a tornado's speed. Based on that information, Khalid then had to calculate the number of miles the storm traveled between its touchdown and retreat.

Kluth & Schwarz

Many interests, like swimming and natural disasters, fit somewhat easily into a math curriculum; others, such as Santa Claus, polka dots, and medieval weapons, may be more difficult to address. In these instances, it can be helpful to simply create materials based on a student's fascination (e.g., a ruler embellished with pictures of Santa Claus) or to use examples that feature favorite characters, objects, or activities. For instance, if a student loves King Kong, the great ape might be featured in test questions or in sample problems, as in the following:

> ✶✭✶ King Kong has to be at the top of the Empire State Building by 9:00 A.M. and it takes him 15 minutes to eat breakfast and 35 minutes to walk to the building. What time should he get up?

> ✶✭✶ When *King Kong* opened at the movie theater, 552 tickets were sold. The second night, 60% fewer tickets were sold. How many tickets were sold the second night?

Gagnon (2001) shared that Jeffrey, a third-grader with Asperger syndrome, also had a fascination that might have been difficult to build into a mathematics curriculum: the World Wrestling Federation. Teachers solved this dilemma by suggesting that he view his multiplication problems as wrestling matches. The problem 55 x 32, for instance, "became the 'five' brothers against the team of 'three and two'" (p. 32).

ADDITIONAL IDEAS FOR BOOSTING MATHEMATICS SKILLS AND COMPETENCIES VIA INTERESTS OR PASSIONS

✦✦✦ Review your mathematics curriculum to find any areas that might intersect well with your students' areas of interest. Be sure to consider all units through the year, as some will certainly fit better than others. It may be hard to generate a variety of ways to incorporate a student's love of antique dollhouses into a unit on probability, but it will be much easier to find these intersections during a study of area and volume.

✦✦✦ Challenge students to bring their interest area into math class. If you cannot think of many ways to enhance math skills and abilities through the use of a learner's fascination, your student might be able to do so. Ask him or her to create a model, write a problem or formula, draw a diagram, or generate a pattern related to his or her area of special interest.

✦✦✦ Try an Internet search of words related to your student's interest area and terms such as *math lessons* or *lesson plans*. You will find math lessons related to telephones, dinosaurs, Native Americans, Ferris wheels, and just about any other passion or hobby you can imagine.

18

To Teach
Manners, Cooperation,
and the Expression of Empathy

In her poignant memoir, *Eating an Artichoke: A Mother's Perspective on Asperger Syndrome* (2000), Echo Fling, the mother of a young man with Asperger syndrome recalls how she taught her son, Jimmy, to interact more sensitively with his sister through lessons she created around Thomas the Tank Engine. Like many young children (with or without autism labels), Jimmy did not always demonstrate empathy in a typical way when others were in need, hurt, or upset. Fling recalled asking Jimmy to comfort his sister when she was crying after hurting her knee. At first, Jimmy simply stared and put his fingers in his ears. When he finally approached his sister, however, his response was not the typical expression of concern. He stood next to her and said simply "a little less noise" (a quote from a favorite movie). This use of language and dead-pan delivery amused Fling, and she immediately saw a teachable moment.

Fling decided to use Jimmy's interest area to teach him a bit about expressing empathy. She began by lining his trains up on the kitchen table and asking Jimmy, "Which one is Thomas?" Once Jimmy picked up the correct toy, Fling proceeded with her lesson. She asked Jimmy if he remembered an episode of his favorite show when Thomas crashed into a pile of snow. Jimmy responded that he did remember and then made a sad face. Fling asked Jimmy what kind of face he was making and he told her, "Sad face." She then questioned him specifically about feelings:

 'Thomas started to cry when the snow covered up his wheels, didn't he.'

'Oh my wheels and coupling rods!' murmured Jimmy.

I knew he had the mental picture of the episode where the little train has an accident and plows right into the snowbank. The dialog was matching perfectly. I decided to make a connection.

'Do you remember when Caroline fell down and hurt her knee this afternoon?' Jimmy nodded. 'She cried, didn't she, just like Thomas.' I waited for his grey matter to finish churning.

'Did Girly feel sad just like Thomas?' he asked.

'Yes, she did.' I answered evenly. Inside my pulse was racing. He was getting it and I didn't want to distract him from the issue with my excitement. I took the next step.

'Do you remember that Terrance the Tractor came to help Thomas out of the snow? That was a nice thing to do. It made Thomas feel better, didn't it?' I waited to see the little Bingo light flash inside his mind.

'Mom?' he asked after a few moments of staring at the trains. 'Do you want me to help Caroline like Terrance helped Thomas?' (p. 75)

Fling found that teaching Jimmy in this manner was so effective she began using it across situations and environments. After learning about concepts such as cooperation, support, and using manners in this way, Jimmy became more aware of how and when he needed to behave differently and was able to demonstrate new skills and competencies.

Fling beautifully illustrates a belief we both hold about people with autism. Although those with autism labels are often characterized as having little or not enough empathy, it is our experience that some of these individuals are the most caring and sensitive people we know. It is our feeling that much of this characterization comes from a struggle that some may have to understand what we (people without autism) *mean* by empathy and how and when it can and should be expressed. Therefore, many students may not need to be taught empathy per se but instead may need help expressing it in typical ways.

The same can be said for teaching manners and etiquette. Individuals on the spectrum may want to be polite but are unaware of social norms. For this reason, students on the spectrum often find learning about manners comforting, as clear and specific rules for behavior can make life less stressful. Students may also like to learn about manners because they are universal in some cases. Rules for opening gifts, greeting people, and sending correspondence vary by region but are enough alike to be comforting for those who struggle with change and novelty. Passions can be easily infused into any curriculum on manners simply by rehearsing scenarios involving the student's area of interest. For instance, Kelly, a student who loved talking about the Appalachian Trail, became interested in learning more about etiquette when his teacher gave him manners guides and hiking literature and asked him to create a guide that hikers could use on the trail. He wrote an excellent manual that included rules such as 1) keep noise to a minimum, 2) take your trash with you when you leave the trail, and 3) travel in small groups. He then worked with a few classmates to create a similar guidebook focusing on rules for the classroom.

ADDITIONAL IDEAS FOR TEACHING MANNERS, COOPERATION, AND THE EXPRESSION OF EMPATHY VIA INTERESTS OR PASSIONS

✦✦ Create minidramas or skits related to etiquette or social norms. Insert the student's fascination by involving his or her favorite characters or by setting a scene that is familiar or preferred. A child who was an avid environmentalist enjoyed learning about social relationships and concepts such as cooperation and sharing when another student dressed up as Mother Nature taught these lessons.

✦✦ If a student's passion, fascination, or special interest is a thing, object, person, or animal, you can discuss the feelings that she, he, or it may have (even if the fascination does not really have feelings, the student may find it helpful to talk about it as if it does) and how to be more respectful, kind, caring, or empathetic to it, her, or him. For instance, if a student loves Curious George, we could ask, "If the Man with the Yellow Hat took a banana away from Curious George, how do you think George would feel?"

✦✦ There are many great manners guides available for children and adolescents, including the following:

Eberly, S. (2001). *365 manners kids should know: Games, activities, and other fun ways to help children learn etiquette.* New York: Three Rivers Press.

Leaf, M. (2002). *How to behave and why.* Riverside, NJ: Universe Publishing.

Packer, A.J. (1997). *How rude! The teenager' guide to good manners, proper behavior, and not grossing people out.* Minneapolis, MN: Free Spirit Publishing.

One way to link student fascinations to the concepts featured in these books is to ask students to write their own manners or classroom rules book featuring a favorite character, concept, place, activity, or hobby.

19

To Encourage Greatness

$\mathcal{F}$or some students, a passion will be a way to pass time, learn, or relax. For others, "enthusiasms" will be their path to remarkable achievement. That is, for some, immersion in a particular area will lead to significant opportunities and perhaps even special recognition. These students, for instance, will end up making noteworthy or even spectacular contributions to business, the arts, industry, sports, science, or other fields.

One such individual is Justin Canha, a teenager with autism who began drawing to supplement his communication as a child. At a very young age, Canha would draw different scenarios to express what had happened to him. The drawings thus served as a bridge to verbal expression, and Canha's parents soon discovered that he had been blessed with an innate artistic talent. Since the age of 5 years, Canha has had a passion for drawing animals and cartoon characters. Today, his body of work includes, among other things, still lifes, landscapes, and portraits in a variety of media, including watercolors, pastels, charcoal, and oils. He has also taught himself computer animation.

Canha has seen many successes in his short life. He participated in a month-long art show at a respected New York art gallery, had his own one-man show the following year, and has even been featured in *O, The Oprah Magazine*. (He also did the cover art for this book because we are such fans of his work and we love how he embodies our message.) This level of attention is extremely unusual for even artists who have worked a lifetime on their art.

Another "star" on the spectrum of autism is Vernon Smith, a big name in the field of economics. Smith has taught at Stanford University, Brown University, and The University of Arizona. His research (and, we suppose, his ability to hyperfocus) has earned him a Nobel Prize, and he has authored or co-authored more than 200 articles and books on capital theory, finance, natural resource economics, and experimental economics.

And Temple Grandin, perhaps the most celebrated and recognized person with autism, is an associate professor at Colorado State University and a world-renowned professional designer of humane livestock facilities. Grandin is considered a philosophical leader of both the animal welfare and autism advocacy movements, as both groups commonly cite her work (and invite her to consult and speak) on issues such as animal welfare, neurology, and philosophy. Grandin, who knows all too well the anxiety of feeling threatened by everything in her surroundings and of being dismissed and feared, has made her mark by championing safe and humane approaches to handling animals. Specifically, she is known for the improvement of standards in slaughter plants and on livestock farms.

Barbara Moran, an artist with autism, sees these types of accomplishments as a result of the "stick-to-it-iveness" of autism.

 I would say if you could take the good qualities, autism itself, if the sensory problems and anxiety are treated, underneath you would find a very smart, very creative person with an open mind. You would probably find somebody who was more of an individualist rather than a conformist. Ordinary people are like sheep; they follow the crowd. The people who've really changed things are people who are different—with freedom.

. . . [T]he fixations of autism [allow us] to stick to something [and] see differently than most people see. [Think of] the big band arrangements, people who write books, you have to be abnormally fixated on something to stick to a big hard job 'til it's done. Because it's amazing what a person can do that's hard if they love to do it. (B. Moran, personal communication, November 9, 2007)

Indeed, Simon Baron-Cohen of the Autism Research Centre at Cambridge University believes that Albert Einstein and Isaac Newton had personalities consistent with Asperger syndrome (Muir, 2003). Although some contest this assessment, Baron-Cohen is not alone in his belief. Many people with autism labels themselves see characteristics in these men that suggest a possible diagnosis. For instance, Einstein and Newton both experienced intense intellectual interests in specific limited areas. They had trouble reacting appropriately in social situations and had difficulty communicating, and both sometimes became so involved with their work that they forgot to eat!

Although only a small percentage of people with autism spectrum labels will achieve this kind of recognition, it serves all teachers well to see that obsessions often can be of great value not only to the person experiencing them but also to others (sometimes to an entire population or culture). It is true, after all, that many of the world's most dazzling accomplishments—including the building of grand structures, scientific discoveries, "firsts" and "bests" in sports and games, and the creation of wonderful art—all require individuals to persevere and to perseverate!

ADDITIONAL IDEAS FOR ENCOURAGING GREATNESS VIA INTERESTS OR PASSIONS

⋆ Encourage students with autism to learn from and about other successful adults who turned their passion into personal or professional success. In addition to studying individuals who have found career success, students can investigate those who became successful by creating something, making a contribution to the community or the world, becoming a leader, or inspiring others.

⋆ Students may be intrigued to learn about the "great" experiences of those with autism and Asperger syndrome. There are many inspiring autobiographies written by successful adults and young people with these labels (see Appendix B for a sample of these resources). Although not all students may attain these authors' type of accomplishments, students may learn a lot from these books about self-acceptance and autistic pride.

⋆ Ask the individual to discuss, write about, or draw how he or she defines "self-greatness," and use this product to inspire and motivate the learner across activities and environments.

20

To Make Life Worth Living

$\mathcal{B}$enji, a high school senior, adores trains and anything to do with the railroad industry. To his delight, he lives less than one block from a major above-ground train track on which run two major city train systems in addition to major national railroad lines. In short, many trains travel these tracks throughout the day. If Benji steps out far enough into his front yard, he is able to see the trains go by. Even more thrilling for Benji are the regular opportunities he has to watch the "train show" on the corner of his block. Whenever he has a chance to do so, he walks down the block, positions himself right by the tracks, and sets up his folding chair and waits in his front-row seat for the entertainment to begin.

When an historic multifamily building across from the train tracks was converted to condominiums, a teacher suggested that Benji might consider eventually moving into the new residences because there are units on the north side that face the tracks. Many would see this type of unit as less preferred, but to Benji it would be heaven. To Benji, the realty mantra "location, location, location" is all about being near the commotion and noise of those trains and being able to have a front row-seat to his favorite "performance" at any time.

Benji's story is just one illustration of how interests can be used to enhance a person's quality of life. And helping people enhance their quality of life is not only kind, it is also potentially a "treatment" for challenging behavior (or what we like to call adventuresome behavior), sagging motivation, and academic or other schooling problems. It may even help alleviate some health concerns such as stress and depression.

Although we may not all share or understand or appreciate how another person becomes inspired or finds contentment, we can certainly try to appreciate that there are "different strokes for different folks." For instance, David Miedzianik (as cited in Attwood, 1998), reported that he finds genuine pleasure in observing a task that to most people would be mundane and unremarkable:

 It always fascinates me watching the gas men mending the stoves. It makes me very excited and I jump up and down when I see the gas flame burning. I've always jumped up and down since I've been a kid. (p. 94)

Too often, "outsiders" see obsessions like Miedzianik's as annoyances or even as problematic, but many people on the autism spectrum identify their fascinations as valuable and desirable. As Joel Smith (2007), an author on the autism spectrum, noted, concentrating on favorites can be incredibly satisfying and pleasurable:

 When I'm interested in something, I might spend so much time immersed in it that I forget to eat or sleep! Many autistics share this characteristic with me, becoming obsessed with what the world might see as unimportant things. I've been asked what it feels like to be immersed in an obsession. It is absolutely wonderful! Time seems to stop, and nothing could bother me while I'm pursuing my "obsession". It doesn't drain me, but it energizes me. I wouldn't give up these "obsessions" for anything. I ask the non-autistics reading this to decide for themselves if there is a problem with someone just because they have an intense passion for something that most people don't enjoy. I wonder how George Washington Carver would have responded if someone told him to quit obsessing over the peanut!

Wendy Lawson (1998) said that she can't imagine a life without her "hyperfocus," a skill and an ability that she has grown to cherish:

 Glancing at the ground as I walked along, I noticed some movement at my feet and saw the last exit moments of a cicada crawling out of a hole in the ground. I watched this creature transform before my eyes from a dull brownish-green bug into a beautiful bright green and gold, singing creation. The process took only one and a half hours. I have since heard that people thought my standing in the heat for one and a half hours to watch an insect was a crazy thing to do. I think it is they who are crazy. By choosing not to stand and watch, they missed out on sharing an experience that was so beautiful and exhilarating. (p. 115)

Jerry Newport, a man with Asperger syndrome who is a math whiz, national speaker, and author of *Your Life is Not a Label* (2001), shares Lawson's perspective and laments the fact that those without autism labels don't seem to understand the joy of just knowing things or the wonder of getting lost in your passion:

I love fans, especially six-blade fans. I hate five-blade fans. I will drive any-where to sit, drink coffee and eat a slice of apple pie in the presence of a row of six-blade fans. I wouldn't walk across the street to be cooled off by a team of five-blade fans if it was 170 degrees.

If you draw a straight line from the tip of each blade to the next tip and do that all around, a six-blade fan fits inside a hexagon. The side of a hexa-gon is equal to the radius of a circle in which a hexagon can be inscribed. Between each pair of blades in a hexagon, you will find an equilateral trian-gle, all sides equal. If you fold each triangle out from the center, you get six more equilateral triangles, twelve in all, within a Star of David, my middle name. Twelve equilateral triangles, one for each tribe of Israel. Not bad insight for a WASP!

It doesn't mean squat, of course, but to me it's cool to know. Why is it so hard for the normals to understand that some things are just cool to know? So cool to know that they can be known all day. (p. 126)

Indeed!

ADDITIONAL IDEAS FOR MAKING LIFE WORTH LIVING VIA INTERESTS OR PASSIONS

★ Educate those in the learner's life about the joy and satisfaction that fascinations can bring. If a student's area of interest is very unusual (and even if it isn't), some people may question what the student "gets" from it and may fail to value or encourage this fascination. Therefore, it can be helpful to let those in the student's life know that some interests do not necessarily have a function or purpose but are there to amuse, delight, or bring joy.

★ Encourage students to advocate for their right to their passions. If students can communicate reliably, you might teach them to educate others about the pleasure they derive from their fascinations. One student we know is often heard telling teachers, "You may not understand it, but please try to accept it."

★ Look for ways to make the student's schooling experiences more enjoyable by providing opportunities to share, spend time with, or reflect on fascinations. When students experience problems or "experience behaviors" at school, attempts frequently are made to correct, address, or even punish the student. Often it is as effective (and sometimes more effective) to build more of students' interests, favorites, or areas of expertise into their daily or weekly experiences. Ask students, "What makes you happy?" and see if you can integrate their responses into their educational experiences. If students cannot share this information, ask their families, "What does your child do when he or she is not at school? How does he or she spend free time?" Most teachers would not think of trying to insert the response "watching the credits from movies" into the school day, but doing so may actually make time at school more exciting, comfortable, and even productive (especially if you can take the credit-viewing experience and turn it into a literacy lesson or into a study of films and related occupations).

References

Aaron, H. (1991). *I had a hammer: The Hank Aaron story.* New York: HarperTorch.

Armstrong, T. (2000). *In their own way: Discovering and encouraging your child's multiple intelligences.* New York: Tarcher.

Armstrong, T. (2002). *You're smarter than you think: A kid's guide to multiple intelligences.* Minneapolis, MN: Free Spirit Publishing.

Armstrong, T. (2003). *The multiple intelligences of reading and writing: Making the words come alive.* Alexandria, VA: Association for Supervision and Curriculum Development.

Attwood, T. (1998). *Asperger's syndrome: A guide for parents and professionals.* Philadelphia: Jessica Kingsley Publishers.

Barron, J., & Barron, S. (1992). *There's a boy in here.* New York: Simon & Schuster.

Berger, M., & Berger, G. (2000). *Brrr! A book about polar animals.* Hempstead, TX: Sagebrush Publishing.

Biklen, D. (2006). *Autism and the myth of the person alone.* New York: Teachers College Press.

Blackman, L. (1999). *Lucy's story: Autism and other adventures.* Philadelphia: Jessica Kingsley Publishers.

Brown, M. (1997). *Stone soup.* New York: Aladdin Books.

Coles, R. (1990). *The call of stories: Teaching and the moral imagination.* Boston: Mariner Books.

Eberly, S. (2001). *365 manners kids should know: Games, activities, and other fun ways to help children learn etiquette.* New York: Three Rivers Press.

Falvey, M.A. (2005). *Believe in my child with special needs! Helping children achieve their potential in school.* Baltimore: Paul H. Brookes Publishing Co.

Fling, E. (2000). *Eating an artichoke: A mother's perspective on Asperger syndrome.* Philadelphia: Jessica Kingsley Publishers.

Gagnon, E. (2001). *Power Cards: Using special interests to motivate children and youth with Asperger syndrome.* Shawnee Mission, KS: Autism Asperger Publishing Company.

Gagnon, E., & Gerland, G. (1997). *A real person: Life on the outside*. London: Souvenir Press.

Gardner, H. (1983). *Frames of mind: The theory of multiple intelligences*. New York: Basic Books.

Gerland, G. (1997). *A real person: Life on the outside*. London: Souvenir Press.

Ginsberg, D. (2002). *Raising Blaze*. New York: Harper Collins.

Grahame, K. (1908) *The wind in the willows*. London: Methuen & Co.

Grandin, T. (1995). *Thinking in pictures*. New York: Vintage Books.

Grandin, T. (2006). *An inside view of autism*. Retrieved September 5, 2007, from http://www.autism.org/temple/inside.html

Grandin, T., & Scariano, M. (1986). *Emergence: Labeled autistic*. Navato, CA: Arena Press.

Gray, C. (2003). *Social Stories 10.0 pdf download*. Kentwood, MI: The Gray Center.

Hall, K. (2001). *Asperger syndrome, the universe and everything*. Philadelphia: Jessica Kingsley Publishers.

Hoff, S. (1992). *Danny and the dinosaur*. New York: HarperCollins.

Holland, O. (2002). *The dragons of autism: Autism as a source of wisdom*. Philadelphia: Jessica Kingsley Publishers.

Hughes, R. (2003). *Running with Walker: A memoir*. Philadelphia: Jessica Kingsley Publishers.

Jackson, L. (2002). *Freaks, geeks, and Asperger syndrome: A user guide to adolescence*. Philadelphia: Jessica Kingsley Publishers.

Kasa-Hendrickson, C., & Kluth, P. (2005). "We have to start with inclusion and work it out as we go": Purposeful inclusion for non-verbal students with autism. *International Journal of Whole Schooling, 2*(1), 2–14.

Kephart, B. (1998). *A slant of sun: One child's courage*. New York: W.W. Norton.

Klin, A., Carter, A., & Sparrow, S.S. (1997). Psychological assessment of children with autism. In D.J. Cohen & F.R. Volkmar (Eds.), *Handbook of autism and pervasive developmental disorders* (2nd ed., pp. 418–427). New York: Wiley.

Kluth, P. (2003). *"You're going to love this kid!": Teaching students with autism in the inclusive classroom*. Baltimore: Paul H. Brookes Publishing Co.

Lawson, W. (1998). *Life behind glass*. Philadelphia: Jessica Kingsley Publishers.

Leaf, M. (2002). *How to behave and why*. Riverside, NJ: Universe Publishing.

Malamud, B. (1952). *The natural*. New York: Farrar, Straus and Giroux.

Marcus, E. (2002, Spring). Compulsion, and yes, freedom too. *Facilitated Communication Digest, 10*(1), 7–10.

Mont, D. (2001). *A different kind of boy: A father's memoir about raising a gifted child with autism*. Philadelphia: Jessica Kingsley Publishers.

Muir, H. (2003, April 30). *Einstein and Newton showed signs of autism.* Retrieved November 20, 2007, from http://www.newscientist.com/article/dn3676.html

Mukhopadhyay, T.R. (2000). *Beyond the silence: My life, the world and autism.* London: National Autistic Society.

Myles, B.S. (2005). *Children and youth with Asperger syndrome.* Thousand Oaks, CA: Corwin Press.

Newport, J. (2001). *Your life is not a label: A guide to living fully with autism and Asperger's syndrome for parents, professionals, and you!* Arlington, TX: Future Horizons.

O'Neill, J.L. (1999). *Through the eyes of aliens: A book about autistic people.* Philadelphia: Jessica Kingsley Publishers.

Packer, A.J. (1997). *How rude! The teenagers' guide to good manners, proper behavior, and not grossing people out.* Minneapolis, MN: Free Spirit Publishing

Park, C. (2002). *Exiting Nirvana: A daughter's life with autism.* Boston: Back Bay Books.

Prince-Hughes, D. (2004). *Songs of the gorilla nation: My journey through autism.* New York: Harmony Books.

Sapon-Shevin, M. (1998). *Because we can change the world: A practical guide to building cooperative, inclusive classroom communities.* Boston: Allyn & Bacon.

Sapon-Shevin, M. (2007). *Widening the circle: The power of inclusive classrooms.* New York: Beacon Press.

Schwarz, P. (2006). *From disability to possibility: The power of inclusive classrooms.* Portsmouth, NH: Heinemann.

Shore, S. (2001). *Beyond the wall: Personal experiences with autism and Asperger syndrome.* Shawnee Mission, KS: Autism Asperger Publishing Company.

Smith, J. (n.d.). *Living with autism: Obsessions. This way of life.* Retrieved August 16, 2007, from http://www.thiswayoflife.org/whatisitlike.html

Tammet, D. (2007). *Born on a blue day: Inside the extraordinary mind of an autistic savant.* New York: Free Press.

Tashie, C., Shapiro-Barnard, S., & Rossetti, Z. (2006). *Seeing the charade: What we need to do and undo to make friendships happen.* Nottingham, United Kingdom: Inclusive Solutions.

Udvari-Solner, A., & Kluth, P. (in press). *Joyful learning: Active and collaborative learning in inclusive classrooms.* Thousand Oaks, CA: Corwin Press.

Waites, J., & Swinbourne, H. (2001). *Smiling at shadows: A mother's journey through heartache and joy.* New York: HarperCollins.

Willey, L.H. (1999). *Pretending to be normal.* Philadelphia: Jessica Kingsley Publishers.

Willey, L.H. (2001). *Asperger syndrome in the family: Redefining normal.* Philadelphia: Jessica Kingsley Publishers.

Williams, D. (1992). *Nobody nowhere: The extraordinary biography of an autistic.* New York: Avon.

Williams, D. (1994). *Somebody, somewhere: Breaking free from the world of autism.* New York: Times Books.

Williams, D. (1996). *Autism: An inside-out approach.* Philadelphia: Jessica Kingsley Publishers.

Winter-Messiers, M.A. (2007). From tarantulas to toilet bowls: Understanding to special interest areas of children and youth with Asperger syndrome. *Remedial and Special Education, 28*(3), 140–152.

Zemelman, S., Daniels, H., & Hyde, A. (2005). *Best practice: Today's standards for teaching and learning in America's schools* (3rd ed.). Portsmouth, NH: Heinemann.

Appendix A
Frequently Asked Questions

 Q *You advocate focusing on student interests, strengths, imagination, and passion areas in this book. Don't you think it is just as important to focus on weaknesses and difficulties?*

A Student files are full of challenge areas because in the current American educational system, this type of information is used to identify learners for special education, in turn helping school districts to qualify these students for services and to receive money for personnel and supports. We understand the need to explore these areas in certain contexts, but we think there is far too much emphasis on student challenges and too little on clearly identifying student interests and passion areas, finding a learning connection, and educating respective individuals accordingly. It is easy to find information about "weaknesses" and "deficits," but this information often provides little concrete guidance on how to support or teach a student; this focus, therefore, becomes a dead end.

Alternatively, delineating and outlining student interests, strengths, goals, and dreams, as well as successful teaching strategies, can help a teacher develop a relationship with the student and effectively plan for and educate him or her. To put it another way, we feel that talking and thinking about students in ways that are more positive, hopeful, and strengths based is not only more kind but also more helpful. On the one hand, when we learn that a child is noncompliant, stubborn, and slow, perseverates on baseball statistics, and is hyperactive, it is hard to imagine how to support him or her. On the other hand, if we learn instead that the student is a self-advocate and sticks up for him- or herself, is careful or cautious, is an expert in calculating and remembering baseball statistics, and is very active and energetic, we have a more positive view of the learner and, we would argue, a better starting point for generating supports and designing instruction.

Q *Doesn't "teaching to passions" really mean "giving in" to the student? Should we really let students perseverate on their obsessions?*

A This is the question we get asked the most often. Our first response is always that it is important to consider how this language (e.g., perseverate, obsession) reflects a negative view of student interests. We suggest that instead of thinking about "giving in" to a student, think about honoring him or her. And instead of thinking about his or her behavior as "perseverating," think about concentrating or being in a state of flow or superfocus.

Furthermore, we challenge our audiences and readers to think about what a useful tool student interests can be to teach social skills, communication skills, relaxation-related skills, and standards-based content and to move students into different areas of study and learning—and thereby potentially into new fascinations. We like to share the example of Ms. Chandler, a high school English teacher who taught us that not only could we value students' areas of interest, we could capitalize on them. When Ms. Chandler learned she would have Raj, a student with autism, in her classroom, she asked many different people (including family members, peers, and previous teachers) for information about him, including his habits, strengths, challenges, and interests. She was told that Raj had only one interest—weather. She was also told that it was impossible to get him to read about, write about, or talk about anything but weather. Ms. Chandler took that as a challenge as she began the year with Raj.

Raj entered Ms. Chandler's classroom on the first day of school and immediately asked her, "What will the weather be today?" Prepared for this question, Ms. Chandler handed Raj the newspaper and showed the young man where he could find the daily weather report in the newspaper each morning. She then told him he could come early to her class each day and write the weather report on the board—the only catch was that he had to use different descriptive words each day to share the information. Over time, she introduced Raj to other sections of the newspaper (including the baseball box scores, which Ms. Chandler read religiously). This led to several in-depth discussions about baseball (with Ms. Chandler occasionally throwing in stories about weather-related disasters at baseball games) that culminated in Raj helping Ms. Chandler design a web site for the school baseball team. In order to be an informed web designer, Ms. Chandler required him to read plenty of informational books about baseball, including *I Had a Hammer: The Hank Aaron Story* (Aaron, 1991) and *The Natural* (Malamud, 1952).

After weeks of helping Raj learn the basics of web design, Ms. Chandler encouraged him to attend meetings of the school's technology club, which ended up being the first extracurricular activity he ever joined (and it wasn't even weather related). At the end of the school year, Raj still loved discussing the weather and had even used his technology know-how to build his own web site, which featured stories, articles, and images of North American natural disasters. However, he also had become interested in baseball and had adopted the Tampa Bay Devil Rays as his team. Furthermore, he had a brand-new passion for technology and web design. Raj accomplished all of this because Ms. Chandler acted on a philosophy to capitalize on student strengths and interests that we can all learn from. Instead of seeing this student's passion as a stumbling block, she saw it as a stepping stone.

A similar stepping-stone-type story comes from the work of Carol Tashie, Susan Shapiro-Barnard, and Zach Rossetti (2006). In *Seeing the Charade,* their stirring book on friendship and inclusion, these educators described a young man named Samuel who had an obsession with fans. He loved to set up fans to blow air across his face or to move things around in space. As teachers sought ways to get Samuel involved in community activities or in extracurricular life, they were hard pressed to find a club of fan lovers. But while searching for hobbies that might be related to fans in some way, a physics teacher referred them to a few students who were building ultralight model planes. This group of youngsters was interested in having Samuel join them in their endeavor, as he had some knowledge of and great interest in wind currents. Samuel, for his part, had the opportunity to learn about aviation, engineering, and building models as a pastime.

As the teachers in these examples illustrate, it can be very helpful to think about student interests as launching pads, springboards, or bridges (Williams, 1996). You can start with a student's passion and consider all of the extensions that might be made into new content areas, interests, skills, and competencies and even into new fascinations. As Ms. Chandler did with Raj, you can build a chainlink of new learning, starting with the student's area of interest as the origin.

 What if it seems impossible for me to link the student's interest area to content, instruction, or supports?

 Nothing is impossible! Einstein said, "Imagination is more important than knowledge," and we agree. Thinking creatively and out of the box can always bring forward innovative solutions. We have known students who have fascinations as obscure and unusual as ball turrets, Rutherford B. Hayes, missile silos, and Branson, Missouri. There are as many student interest areas as there are students, and this goes for both individuals who have and do not have autism.

If you truly feel you are at a standstill for incorporating the interest area into the curriculum, start with an Internet search on the topic or consider having the respective student conduct such a search. This method can lead you to web sites, resources, organizations, and, of course, other people with ideas for creating links to learning in the classroom.

If a web search doesn't yield enough and you still cannot see connections to curriculum, instruction, supports, or classroom environment, you might stick with options that allow the learner to pursue the area of interest on his or her own. Research projects, extra credit opportunities, independent studies, mentorships, and internships are all options. Teachers might also consider going outside the classroom to inspire learners. Students' interests might be explored via field trips, community groups, or even local and national conferences. Tashie, Shapiro-Barnard, and Rossetti (2006) shared a story of a man with a passion for collecting air sirens. Because this is a rather unique interest, the man had to look outside his community for connections and therefore went all the way to Moscow to attend the International Air Siren Convention(!), illustrating that there truly is something for everyone. No matter what a student loves, there are probably others elsewhere (somewhere) who love it, too, and where there is a will to teach, connect to, support, extend, or build a bridge from a student's passion, there is certainly a way.

 I know it is important to be positive and to honor the things students love, but what if they get really carried away with their fascination? Is it ever okay to try and move the child away from his favorites?

 Although it may be useful to negotiate how and when students engage in their fascinations, students will most likely do their best work and find the most success when we seek ways to integrate them into the day. Students often need favorite materials, activities, behaviors, and interest areas to relax, focus, or make connections with others. Even if we cannot see how it works or happens, students with autism are often using their interests to serve some purpose, even if it is to escape difficulty, regain composure, find a moment of solitude, or enjoy beauty.

Donna Williams (1996), in fact, believes that accepting and building on fascinations and fixations can be good not only for people with autism but also for those without it:

> It may be more advantageous to meet and share with these 'autistic' people on territory that does make sense to them than to take away the only things that do hold significance for them in favour of compliance. Some [individuals] really need to ask themselves whether they might not be able to have a little more tolerance of eccentricity than they already have, not just regarding the 'autistic' people in their care, but in themselves as well. (p. 229)

Having shared this sentiment, however, it is important to note that some individuals with autism may occasionally express a desire to spend less time with or even to get rid of a passion. In these instances, the teacher should support the student in doing so. Yet, it is important to emphasize that this process should be done in respectful ways and always in collaboration with the student.

More tricky is the situation in which the teacher makes a decision that the interest area must be limited or "extinguished." We believe if the student is not interested in moving away from their fascination area, the teacher should proceed with caution and carefully evaluate this decision. Eugene Marcus (2002), a writer, teacher, and advocate who has autism, indicated that fascinations and interests often serve important purposes in his life and that although they sometimes get in the way or cause him struggle, he feels that *he* must be the one "managing" his fixations; furthermore, some of the challenges of his so-called compulsions also hold lessons:

> My own view is that my life is enriched and made livable by the habits that enslave me. My feeling is that my enslavement is a voluntary one in that nobody else forces me to be compulsive, or even gives me permission to be compulsive.
>
> My wish is to one day be free of my compulsions, but not any day soon. By being an inconvenient and loud slave to compulsion, I have learned things I never would have through silent cooperation. I have tested the limits of my real and unreal friends (even those people who wanted to be my friends, but only when I was play-acting a role—not being myself). My compulsive behavior has allowed me to set my own agenda in situations where the most I could have hoped for was "eats and treats." My compulsive behav-

ior is a long-playing defense against well meaning people who cannot guess what I really am thinking of or wishing for. (p. 8)

Marcus goes on to share that the way to help those with compulsions may be to stop implementing procedures and programs that are oppressive and to support the individual in finding a variety ways to be in control of his or her own life:

Compulsiveness can be a useful weapon, but like all weapons it can be misused. I look forward to burying my weapons someday and traveling unarmed through the world. Maybe then people will see the man behind the armor more easily. Some day, we will all disarm. I will drop my compulsiveness when my staff decide to drop their desire to keep me under control. (p. 8)

Liane Holliday Willey (2001), a woman with Asperger syndrome, suggests having frank and serious conversations about the "good and bad parts of obsessing" (p. 125) instead of trying to change people and get them to quit their passions. She shared how she has helped her daughter, who also has Asperger syndrome, learn to live in concert with her interests:

Slowly, patiently, with tiny steps, we are trying to help her find the good and the bad parts of obsessing. "It is good to play with your monkey collection when you feel badly about something that happened at school," we tell her. "Of course you can buy that book about monkeys because you worked hard to control your temper this whole week," we will say. "No, you cannot sort your monkeys right now, not until your homework is finished," we remind her. In time, she will do these things for herself. In time she will know on her own how to share her life with her obsessions. (p. 125)

This caring approach can, of course, also be used with students who are nonverbal. Do not limit time with passions without letting an individual know when, where, and under which circumstances he or she can gain access to preferred experiences or materials again. Always educate students about why breaks from certain experiences are necessary; this means talking to students who may not be able to respond. Be gentle and sincere in all of these instances, and let students know that you realize how much their passions mean to them.

In other words, if you must limit, do it with grace, kindness, and creativity. Barbara Moran, a colleague and friend of ours who has vivid recollections of her childhood fascinations squelched in ways that were not graceful, kind, or creative, asked us to remind teachers to never "yank away a child's cathedral" (her passion), as this approach is not only cruel but also ineffective (B. Moran, personal communication, November 9, 2007). She remembers that her interest was never valued and sometimes punished. According to Moran, this is ironic because "I would have done any darn thing they wanted if they just would have given me pictures of cathedrals to gaze at throughout the day."

 How does this idea of using passions as springboards or stepping stones apply to families? How can parents do this at home?

It probably will not surprise our readers to learn that many of these ideas came from families. Mothers and fathers who know and love their children often figure out how to do this work of "exploiting" passions before the teacher does. This happens most likely because parents have the opportunity to support their children across many environments and because they have a deep sense of how important and even sacred some of these "enthusiasms" are to their children.

Many of the ideas we share throughout this book translate easily to home and community environments. The examples we give for using interests in the standards-based curriculum, for instance, can also be used in Sunday school, and the ideas shared for preparing the inclusive classroom can be implemented in the student's bedroom or in the family home. One mother we know used these ideas to both bolster her son's leisure time activities and to bring the family closer together. This testimonial comes from an e-mail she sent to us after learning about the give-him-the-whale concept:

> I've got a son 'stuck' on front loading washers and dryers. I'm embarrassed to say how much time is spent trying to distract him from the basement when laundry's going. I've been contemplating putting a lock on the basement door, but he's now taller and certainly smarter than I, so what's the point?

She went on to share that after attending our seminar on honoring fascinations, she came home and searched for a magazine her son had been dragging around the house, thinking it had an advertisement for front loading machines but she was mistaken:

> Turns out it was a five page article on re-decorating your laundry room. I started reading him the article and as I'm sure you're not surprised to hear, he was thrilled. When I'm old and grey sitting in my rocker, I will remember this moment as one of my favorites! Then we pulled out all the pages, so we could save them, and started talking about the sizes and colors of baskets, machines, and laundry accessories—who knew? We even decided that when

Grandpa returns from Florida next month we will have him help us redecorate the laundry room. That upped the excitement quotient! Then I pulled my husband aside and although he was skeptical, I talked him into finding the owner's manuals and the DVD for the machine. My son was so thrilled; you would have thought it was Christmas. No, let me correct that, he has never been as excited about a Christmas or birthday gift. So, I'm planning to stop by Home Depot and Best Buy and get as many ads, brochures, and manuals as we can find, and use a front loading washer and dryer to teach every concept I can come up with!

Clearly, families have the ability not only to apply these concepts at home but also to teach educators how to engage in this work. It is our hope that the ideas in this book will inspire new home–school collaboration and give opportunities for teams to design, in addition to powerful curriculum and instruction, supports for school and home and opportunities for students to grow, learn, and find happiness within and beyond school walls.

 At my school, we use student fascinations as rewards for good behavior and not as tools for teaching and supporting. Changing this practice would be a struggle for us. How do you get your colleagues to change their way of thinking?

If students are able to engage in their major fascination or interest area only as a reward for good behavior, the bar often can be too high and, for many, unreachable. If the student does not achieve or loses his or her reward, the entire day can be ruined, causing anger, sadness, or depression. Therefore, the reward that was originally created to reinforce the student ceases to do so, creating a punishment (and many times behavior that escalates further). For this reason, we commend you for your interest in challenging an entrenched and often damaging practice in special education.

We know that bringing a new idea to colleagues and getting buy-in is not always easy. Initially, not everyone may be thrilled to try something new, but if you can position these fascination-based strategies as fun to develop or as out of the box, fresh, or even radical, colleagues who like to be on the cutting edge or those who value ingenuity may be more inclined to experiment with them.

You also can try asking your colleagues to think about their own lives and experiences. Remind them that the simplest reason to use student fascinations as tools for teaching and supporting is that all people, regardless of age, work best when they have activities, responsibilities, and expectations during their day that involve an area about which they feel passionate! Many people without disabilities (especially those who have ever had a bad job experience) can relate to the need for motivation and inspiration in the course of the day.

Finally, you can try appealing to your team by sharing information about best practice in education. In the popular book *Best Practice: Today's Standards for Teaching and Learning in America's Schools, Third Edition,* Zemelman, Daniels, and Hyde (2005) concluded that the curriculum for any student should allow for ongoing choice and input in the areas of assignments, activities, and projects. Therefore, empowering students in their own learning enterprise through interest areas, fascinations, and passions is supported by research and is a practice recommended by leaders in science, social studies, math, language arts, and other subject areas.

 Q ***If I give my student time with his or her passion and fascination during the school day, how do I get him or her away from it when it is time to make the transition to other things?***

A Many students who have a favorite interest area that is explored in school may have a difficult time leaving their time spent in this "wow" experience. By providing students some choices about how they use their time for particular periods of the day and allowing some flexibility in when and where they will incorporate their favorites, teachers may keep students more calm and relaxed and find that struggles are kept to a minimum. If a student requires visual supports or teaching strategies to transition away from his or her special activities, materials, or topics, tools can be built into the day for this purpose. Effective tools or strategies include but are not limited to using a schedule (words or pictures or both), a timer, brief reminders about the duration of the time with favorites (written, pictorial, or verbal), and specifications about how and when the individual will be able to revisit his or her fascination.

Also consider secondary interests that are reinforcing to the student, allowing time for those as well. After the student's most preferred activity of the day, you might offer some time related to a secondary interest to ensure a smoother transition and acceptance of the next activity. Also, as we discuss throughout the book, embedding the topic throughout different subject and activity areas may ease transitions. For example, if Tania is passionate about *The Wizard of Oz,* she will adore spending time reading the book and maybe even the screenplay or creating a poster of the good and evil characters and healthy/nonhealthy relationships that are depicted in both the book and movie.

In mathematics, she could use character names for the numeric story problem; for science, many areas could be related to concepts in the book such as chemicals (potions), inventions (hot air balloons), and nature (storms). As students become more comfortable in the classroom and feel safe enough to take risks, they may require fewer references and connections to their area of passion. The more frequently we use their interests as ways to connect to new content, the easier it will be to introduce novelty into their educational experiences.

 What if my student's interest changes? Will the fascination likely be lifelong?

As with any of us with a particular deep interest, it may remain or it may change and evolve. No matter what the particular passion a student has currently, the strategies and examples in this book will help you to accept, embrace, promote, and further develop the relationship it has to school activities and the curriculum. Opening the doors to the fascination and supporting the student in exploring new interests as they evolve is what effective teaching is all about. For example, we have just learned that the student who inspired us to write this book, Pedro, has chosen a new interest area. He has evolved from being passionate about whales to being passionate about windmills (perhaps the sequel to this book should be titled *Just Give Him the Generator!*). A wise and knowing teacher will put forward the philosophy "Change is good" by introducing new opportunities, ways, and means for Pedro to explore windmills in the curriculum. Windmills, generators, and engines may be embedded into Pedro's curriculum as whales were before, and, once again, other learners in his classroom community can be encouraged to provide supports as they did with Pedro's first interest. If whales evolve into a secondary passion for Pedro, they may also continue in the curriculum as well, depending on his needs and desires. Once this approach is utilized for a student, it gets easier when doing it again for the same student or others in the classroom. Keeping your eyes, your ears, and your mind open will undoubtedly result in new ideas for all learners and make it more likely that you will be that unforgettable teacher who not only teaches and supports but inspires!

Appendix B

ADDITIONAL RESOURCES FOCUSED ON STRENGTHS, ABILITIES, AND INTERESTS

AUTOBIOGRAPHIES WRITTEN BY PEOPLE WITH AUTISM AND ASPERGER SYNDROME

Undoubtedly, the best way to learn about autism is to learn from people who have it. Fortunately, people with autism are sharing their experiences in increasing numbers. Teachers who want to prepare to have students with autism in their classrooms or those who want to learn more about those already in their schools have a variety of books to choose from, including autobiographies of individuals with autism and Asperger syndrome, "how-to" guides for teaching, and books written specifically for young people on the autism spectrum. Some of our favorites are included here.

Blackman, L. (1999). *Lucy's story: Autism and other adventures.* Philadelphia: Jessica Kingsley Publishers.

Blackman's memoir is entertaining and filled with great family stories, insight into how she learns, and helpful hints on supporting people with significant disabilities. Throughout her story, Blackman reminds the reader of her many abilities, including her knack for literacy learning.

Gerland, G. (1997). *A real person: Life on the outside.* London: Souvenir Press.

Gerland's story is poignant. Her accounts of personal relationships are especially honest and offer a window into some of the struggles and gifts of people with autism attributes.

Grandin, T. (1995). *Thinking in pictures: My life with autism.* New York: Vintage Books.

Grandin's most popular autobiographical text is filled with examples of how her teachers and family members recognized her abilities early on and encouraged her to develop her many talents. A primary focus of this text is how her ability to "think in pictures" has brought her success.

Grandin, T., & Scariano, M. (1986). *Emergence: Labeled autistic.* Navato, CA: Arena Press.

Grandin's first book, like her others, is a fascinating read. She constantly implores the reader to look to the strengths of individuals with autism and provides many examples of how her interests in livestock, science, and math led her to her chosen career path.

Hall, K. (2001). *Asperger syndrome, the universe and everything.* Philadelphia: Jessica Kingsley Publishers.

This book is not only a quick and easy read but appropriate for students as well as teachers. Written by Hall when he was only 10 years old, it is an account of both student life and the personal journey of life with Asperger syndrome. It is both funny and insightful and will give the reader many practical hints on how to teach and support learners and their many passions.

Jackson, L. (2002). *Freaks, geeks, and Asperger syndrome: A user guide to adolescence.* Philadelphia: Jessica Kingsley Publishers.

We highly recommend this book to anyone who asks us about teaching students with Asperger syndrome. Jackson wrote this as a teenager, and it is directed toward young people and those trying to understand people on the spectrum. Jackson, who is crazy about computers, among other things, implores us all to have more reverence for student fascinations.

Lawson, W. (1998). *Life behind glass.* Philadelphia: Jessica Kingsley Publishers.

In this short, user-friendly guide, Lawson reflects on some of the struggles in her life as well as the many delights of being on the autism spectrum.

Mukhopadhyay, T.R. (2000). *Beyond the silence: My life, the world and autism.* London: National Autistic Society.

Mukhopadhyay, a gifted writer, shares his perspective and his wonderful poetry throughout this short but meaningful volume. His schooling experiences, both the positive and the negative, are chronicled in this book, as are his views on autism, teaching, and support.

Newport, J. (2001). *Your life is not a label: A guide to living fully with autism and Asperger's syndrome for parents, professionals, and you!* Arlington, TX: Future Horizons.

The title says it all! This guide is a great read for people who love, care about, or support those with autism labels, but it also may be most useful for those on the autism spectrum. In a style that can be seen as both gentle and straightforward, Newport encourages those with labels to live life fully and celebrate difference.

O'Neill, J.L. (1999). *Through the eyes of aliens: A book about autistic people.* Philadelphia: Jessica Kingsley Publishers.

This book can be seen as a guide for "neurotypicals." O'Neill's story is beautifully written and repeatedly sends the powerful message, "Respect us. Try and understand."

Prince-Hughes, D. (2004). *Songs of the gorilla nation: My journey through autism.* New York: Harmony Books.

A compelling account of growing up and self-discovery but also a fascinating look at how an "obsession" can become the focus and love of one's life. Prince-Hughes shares in detail how a love of gorillas turned into her life's work.

Shore, S. (2001). *Beyond the wall: Personal experiences with autism and Asperger syndrome.* Shawnee Mission, KS: Autism Asperger Publishing Company.

Shore's book is a great choice for those learning about autism for the first time. It is funny, touching, and easy to read, as Shore is both a person on the autism spectrum and a teacher himself. Teaching to interests is a theme of this book and Stephen himself admits to having fascinations as wide ranging as music, yoga, cats, and autism.

Tammet, D. (2007). *Born on a blue day: A memoir.* New York: Free Press.

Tammet's autobiography is a very humble account of a man with a remarkable mathematical mind. Celebrated in the documentary *Brainman,* Tammet is a "human calculator" and can solve a wide range of mathematical problems in just seconds. In this very open account, we learn about the author's many loves, including chess, ladybugs, libraries, and, of course, numbers.

Willey, L.H. (1999). *Pretending to be normal.* Philadelphia: Jessica Kingsley Publishers.

We recommend Willey's book widely, as it is honest and even poetic. It is filled with anecdotes, stories, and examples of how "normal" is a state of mind. Willey implores those without autism to see the gifts that may be associated with human diversity.

Williams, D. (1992). *Nobody nowhere: The extraordinary biography of an autistic.* New York: Avon.

Williams chronicles many of her struggles in this, her most celebrated autobiographical work, yet we also learn about her keen self-awareness, her artistic abilities, and her knack for storytelling and writing.

Williams, D. (1996). *Autism: An inside-out approach.* Philadelphia: Jessica Kingsley Publishers.

Although this book is not really an autobiography, it is a gem written by a woman who is a seasoned writer, great communicator, and person who understands the needs of young people with autism and Asperger syndrome. This book has been invaluable in our own work with students and with families. It discusses everything from communication to connection to sensory issues, supporting student passions.

AUTOBIOGRAPHIES WRITTEN BY FAMILIES OF PEOPLE WITH AUTISM AND ASPERGER SYNDROME

Families of individuals with autism are publishing personal accounts more than ever before. Teachers can learn so much from the perspective of families, who see and can so often elegantly share their child's gifts, skills, abilities, and strengths. Although dozens (and maybe hundreds) of these accounts are now available and they all have something to offer the field, we are sharing those that have a particular focus on honoring fascinations and uniqueness.

Fling, E. (2000). *Eating an artichoke: A mother's perspective on Asperger syndrome*. Philadelphia: Jessica Kingsley Publishers.

This family story is one we share with parents and teachers alike. Fling's story of her son, Jimmy, focuses not only on how families can positively support those with autism labels but how they can appreciate and honor them, too.

Ginsberg, D. (2002). *Raising Blaze*. New York: Harper Collins.

Ginsberg is a mother committed to seeking and capitalizing on her son's strengths. This is a lovely story of a mother's (and a very committed grandfather's) optimistic outlook.

Holland, O. (2002). *The dragons of autism: Autism as a source of wisdom*. Philadelphia: Jessica Kingsley Publishers.

When a child is diagnosed with autism, many parents first react with fear and hopelessness. Holland felt this way when her son, Billy, was diagnosed; instead of giving up hope, however, she developed strategies to support him. Since then, she and her family have come to see some of autism's blessings. In this uplifting family story, Holland explains how working with the many strengths of autism has led to a better quality of life for her family.

Hughes, R. (2003). *Running with Walker: A memoir.* Philadelphia: Jessica Kingsley Publishers.

Hughes's son does not have reliable communication and cannot show what he knows, but this father shares, in many different ways, how he sees his son's abilities in the midst of all of his difficulties. Building on this view of his son, Hughes chronicles how he teaches his child about architecture, urban life, animals, and the love of family.

Kephart, B. (1998). *A slant of sun: One child's courage.* New York: W.W. Norton.

In radiant prose, Kephart shares her experience of loving her creative and one-of-a-kind son. In this text, the author asks the questions, "Is normal possible? Can it be defined? . . . And is normal superior to what the child inherently is, to what he aspires to, fights to become, every second of his day?"

Mont, D. (2001). *A different kind of boy: A father's memoir about raising a gifted child with autism.* Philadelphia: Jessica Kingsley Publishers.

Monts's story is very touching and just as humorous. His son Alex is an amazing child prodigy in math and one of seven fourth-graders in the United States to ace the National Math Olympiad. *A Different Kind of Boy* is a sweet story of a father helping his talented son make sense of the world while encouraging his many fascinations.

Waites, J., & Swinbourne, H. (2001). *Smiling at shadows: A mother's journey through heartache and joy.* New York: HarperCollins.

This family account out of Australia is unique in that Waites wrote it after her child was grown. The lessons she learned in raising Dane, her adult son with autism, are told with great sensitivity and pride.

Willey, L.H. (2001). *Asperger syndrome in the family: Redefining normal.* Philadelphia: Jessica Kingsley Publishers.

One of our very favorite reads, Willey writes as not only a parent of a child with Asperger syndrome but as an Aspie herself. The result is a two-for-one experience, in which readers get the perspective of not only a person on the autism spectrum but also of a loving and strengths-focused mother who looks for the abilities in all three of her children and teaches them to be advocates.

OTHER STRENGTHS-FOCUSED RESOURCES

Other resources we recommend and use ourselves when teaching about strengths, fascinations, and gifts are described here. Some of these resources are written for teachers, but all would be helpful for families and educators alike.

Armstrong, T. (2000). *In their own way: Discovering and encouraging your child's multiple intelligences.* New York: Tarcher.

This is a great primer on applying the multiple intelligences model. The book challenges labels such as "unmotivated," "hyper," and "noncompliant," and the author explains how these labels focus on deficits when what we really need to be doing is exploring *how* kids are smart.

Armstrong, T. (2002). *You're smarter than you think: A kid's guide to multiple intelligences.* Minneapolis, MN: Free Spirit Publishing.

We really like this user-friendly resource written for students. It communicates what so many young people need to hear in this age of testing and standardization: Everyone learns differently and is unique. Armstrong devotes a chapter to each of the eight different intelligences—word, music, logic, picture, body, people, self, and nature—and describes each in a way that kids can understand.

Armstrong, T. (2003). *The multiple intelligences of reading and writing: Making the words come alive.* Alexandria, VA: Association for Supervision and Curriculum Development.

This book examines the intersection of the multiple intelligences model and reading instruction and explores how we can reach a wider range of learners by attending to what each student does well. For example, Armstrong suggests that teachers use songs and rhythms to teach spelling, punctuation, and vocabulary to those who respond better to music than to words.

Biklen, D. (2006). *Autism and the myth of the person alone.* New York: Teachers College Press.

Biklen and a host of individuals with autism collaborated on this project, sharing a variety of stories about life with autism. Although not all are focused specifically on strengths and passions, the tone of the book is overwhelmingly positive and respectful.

Coles, R. (1990). *The call of stories: Teaching and the moral imagination.* Boston: Mariner Books.

Calling upon his own memories and experiences, Coles delivers a beautiful book about the transformative power of stories and the need to listen to those we purport to help. Written primarily for physicians, this is a very useful text for anyone in a helping profession.

Falvey, M.A. (2005). *Believe in my child with special needs! Helping children achieve their potential in school.* Baltimore: Paul H. Brookes Publishing Co.

This book is helpful and ever so hopeful. Falvey's orientation to teaching, learning, and collaboration is incredibly positive and student centered. She encourages the reader to look for the gifts in all learners.

Kluth, P. (2003). *"You're going to love this kid!": Teaching students with autism in the inclusive classroom.* Baltimore: Paul H. Brookes Publishing Co.

"You're Going to Love this Kid!" is focused on inclusive education and building on learners' successes. As in *"Just Give Him the Whale!"*, Paula emphasizes listening to and learning from learners and building on competencies and abilities.

Sapon-Shevin, M. (1998). *Because we can change the world: A practical guide to building cooperative, inclusive classroom communities.* Boston: Allyn & Bacon.

This book delivers promise and practical goals for teachers who wish to create a warm, respectful, and nurturing learning environment for their students. *Because We Can Change the World* helps teachers show children how to understand and accept differences among themselves and in the world in a way that empowers them to make a difference. This book includes plenty of lesson ideas, including cooperative games, children's literature selections and activities, and songs that establish a supportive environment.

Sapon-Shevin, M. (2007). *Widening the circle: The power of inclusive classrooms.* New York: Beacon Press.	This work embraces individual differences in the classroom and brings forward practices to forge success for all. Strategies include universal accessibility of teaching activities and materials, students teaching one another, and innovative projects that spark teaching and learning. Ideas from real classrooms across the country are provided throughout.
Schwarz, P. (2006). *From disability to possibility: The power of inclusive classrooms.* Portsmouth, NH: Heinemann.	Through use of real-life stories about learners from "womb to tomb," Patrick's book provides components of a model entitled "possibility studies." By focusing on learner attributes and outcomes, this book shows how the fields of special education and human services can be inspired to strengthen practices that can create positive outcomes and reform practices that are not effectively serving learners.
Zemelman, S., Daniels, H., & Hyde, A. (2005). *Best practice: Today's standards for teaching and learning in America's schools* (3rd ed.). Portsmouth, NH: Heinemann.	The authors of this important work examined national curriculum reports since the mid-1980s for educational recommendations that teachers should be promoting in schools and other educational techniques that teachers should be avoiding. Learner diversity is the focus here, with collaboration between general and special educators emphasized as an essential practice to achieving educational success.